A Prisoner in the Garden

THE NELSON MANDELA FOUNDATION

VIKING STUDIO

VIKING STUDIO

Published by the Penguin Group

Penguin Group (USA) Inc., 375 Hudson Street, New York, New York 10014, U.S.A.

Penguin Group (Canada), 90 Eglinton Avenue East, Suite 700, Toronto, Ontario, Canada M4P 2Y3 (a division of Pearson Penguin Canada Inc.)

Penguin Books Ltd, 80 Strand, London WC2R 0RL, England

Penguin Ireland, 25 St. Stephen's Green, Dublin 2, Ireland (a division of Penguin Books Ltd)

Penguin Books Australia Ltd, 250 Camberwell Road, Camberwell, Victoria 3124, Australia (a division of Pearson Australia Group Pty Ltd)

Penguin Books India Pvt Ltd, 11 Community Centre, Panchsheel Park, New Delhi – 110 017, India

Penguin Group (NZ), Cnr Airborne and Rosedale Roads, Albany, Auckland 1310, New Zealand (a division of Pearson New Zealand Ltd)

Penguin Books (South Africa) (Pty) Ltd, 24 Sturdee Avenue, Rosebank, Johannesburg 2196, South Africa

Penguin Books Ltd, Registered Offices: 80 Strand, London WC2R 0RL, England

First American edition

Published in 2006 by Viking Studio, a member of Penguin Group (USA) Inc.

10   9   8   7   6   5   4   3   2   1

Copyright © Nelson Mandela Foundation, 2005

All rights reserved

ISBN 0-670-03753-2

Printed in the United Kingdom by Butler And Tanner Ltd, Frome

Set in Corporate 9.5 / 14

Designed by Flame Design, Cape Town, South Africa

Acknowledgements

This book is the result of a collective endeavour spearheaded by the Nelson Mandela Foundation's Nelson Mandela Centre of Memory and Commemoration Project. Project team members are Verne Harris (Project Manager), Anthea Josias, Boniswa Qabaka, Buyi Sishuba, Ethel Arends and Mayra Roffe Gutman.

The project is given strategic direction by a steering committee comprising Nelson Mandela Foundation staff members and Minister Pallo Jordan, Professor Njabulo Ndebele, Ahmed Kathrada, André Odendaal and Heiko Roehl. The Chairperson of this committee is John Samuel.

We acknowledge with gratitude the work undertaken by the following teams:
Writing: Carolyn Hamilton (lead writer), Verne Harris, Mac Maharaj and Anthea Josias
Design: Clive van den Berg (lead designer) and Nabeel Essa
Curation: Lauren Segal (lead curator) and Anthea Josias
Research: Anthea Josias (lead researcher), Lauren Segal,
Mayra Roffe Gutman and Carolyn Hamilton
Specialist advice: Ahmed Kathrada, Mac Maharaj and Kerry Harris
The Penguin South Africa team, led by Jeremy Boraine, has been a pleasure to work with. Their high quality of editing and design support was unwavering. Instrumental to the Penguin input were Flame Design (designer Marius Roux) and editor Sean Fraser.

We are also grateful to all the institutions that offered assistance and support in locating records. In particular, we acknowledge the crucial role played by the National Archives in facilitating access, partnering the Nelson Mandela Foundation in the 466/64: A Prisoner Working in the Garden exhibition, and giving permission for the reproduction of official documentation. Many individuals within these institutions and beyond gave willingly of their time and expertise. The inputs of Zahira Adams, Gail Behrman, Ingrid Gavshon, Natalie Skomolo and Gerrit Wagener deserve special mention.

Anthony Sampson's authorised biography, *Mandela* (HarperCollins Publishers, 1999), has been a reliable point of reference. And we thank historian Cornelius Thomas for sharing his research on the notebooks returned to Mandela by Donald Card.

Of course, our inspiration has been Madiba himself. His support for this book project was an invaluable asset.

Verne Harris
Nelson Mandela Foundation

TABLE OF CONTENTS

Foreword

In the life of any individual, family, community or society, memory is of fundamental importance. It is the fabric of identity. This is something those who devised and imposed apartheid on South Africa knew well. At the heart of every oppressive tool developed by the apartheid regime was a determination to control, distort, weaken, even erase people's memories. For those of us who spent many years in prison, this attack on memory was felt deep within us, actually in our bodies – the physical yearning to touch loved ones, breathe in the smells of home, feel the texture of a favourite jersey. The struggle against apartheid can be typified as the pitting of remembering against forgetting. It was in our determination to remember our ancestors, our stories, our values and our dreams that we found comradeship. As has been known and practised in our country for many centuries, the memory of an individual is founded in collective memory, and it is with this ancient wisdom in mind that we inaugurated the Nelson Mandela Centre of Memory and Commemoration Project. It is the task of the Centre to continue to unravel the many silences imposed by our apartheid and colonial pasts, to find space for the memories suppressed by power.

We have mandated the Centre to locate and document – and facilitate public access to – the many archives that contain traces of my life and those who have lived it with me. The Centre's first major project involved unlocking what it calls the Prison Archive. This book tells the story of that project, a story made up of many stories. Anyone who has explored the world of archives will know that it is a treasure house, one that is full of surprises, crossing paths, dead ends, painful reminders and unanswered questions. Very often, the memories contained in archives diverge from the memories people carry with them. That is its challenge. And its fascination.

Engagement with archives offers both joy and pain. The experience of viewing my prison archive has been a personal one for me. Readers are invited to share in it.

NR Mandela

One Man's Memory – Nelson Mandela Previews the Exhibition

It is 13 August 2004, and the Nelson Mandela Centre of Memory project team is finalising preparations for the launch of the 466/64: A Prisoner Working in the Garden exhibition. An audience with Nelson Mandela has been arranged to brief him and to share some of the materials to be put on display. In attendance is photographer Matthew Willman, whose photo essay on Robben Island is to be an important element of the exhibition.

Mandela listens attentively to the explanation offered by the project manager. As Willman gets in close, Mandela's personal assistant Zelda la Grange notices a loose hair on his shoulder and leans forward to brush it off. He smiles: 'They just fall out, you know. There is nothing you can do about it.'

When the documents and photographs are presented to him, he examines each one in turn, first silently then in a flow of reminiscence. His curiosity is palpable, and the stories abound. He pauses longest over the collection of images from the 1977 visit to Robben Island by a select group of journalists.

'I remember that day,' he says. 'The authorities brought these people to prove that we were still alive.' When preparing his autobiography *Long Walk to Freedom* ten years earlier, Mandela had forgotten about this media visit. A note of anger creeps into his voice as he denounces one of the individuals on the visit. La Grange admonishes him: 'Khulu [Great One], you know you can't talk like that...'
'No,' he responds, 'we must be honest about these things.'

He holds the portrait of himself, also taken on the 1977 visit, for several minutes. The project manager alerts him to the Prison Service caption on the reverse side, which states in Afrikaans 'A prisoner working in the garden'.

Mandela interrupts: 'You should have let me read it. I could have shown off that I can speak proper Afrikaans.'

Finally, a 2004 birthday gift from former fellow-prisoner Mac Maharaj is presented to him. It is a framed copy of the *National Geographic* photograph his fellow prisoners had given Mandela as a birthday gift on Robben Island 40 years before. He chuckles as he views the image of an exuberant young woman running naked on a beach.

'Ah yes, I remember this well...' And then, after a pause, 'We are not ashamed of these things.'
The audience is over. As the project manager packs away the materials, Mandela holds onto the *National Geographic* photograph. 'Can I keep it?' he asks.

Johannesburg.
18 July 2004.

Dear Madiba,

In the early seventies, when you were still a young man and when we were still not allowed in our cells photos of our loved ones, we came across this picture in the National Geographic. It is a photo of an Andamanese woman running effortlessly on the beach – a glorious celebration of life.

You fell in love with the photo. I used a broken blade to carve a frame from a tomato box plank. We gave you the framed picture as a birthday present. You kept it on your bookshelf. The regime got the press to photograph your cell in 1978. And there in the media was splashed your bookcase (made out of cardboard) & this framed photo (which the press said was Winnie!). Little did they know of this secret love of yours!

Not many know that the Andaman Islands lie east of India and are populated by African people. It remains unexplained how and when they got there. Few too know that the Andaman Islands were, under the British, the Robben Island for Indian "terrorists".

And so, having traced the National Geographic of the late sixties/early seventies, I thought we would frame it much like the one we gave you in prison, and give it to you on this your 86th birthday to share with aunt Graca and the family as a remembrance of a little thing that brought beauty and hope into a desolate cell 30-35 years ago.

Happy birthday & may you in the bosom of you family have a truly wonderful and joyous day.

                    Mac
                    and Zarina, Milou and Sekai Jo.

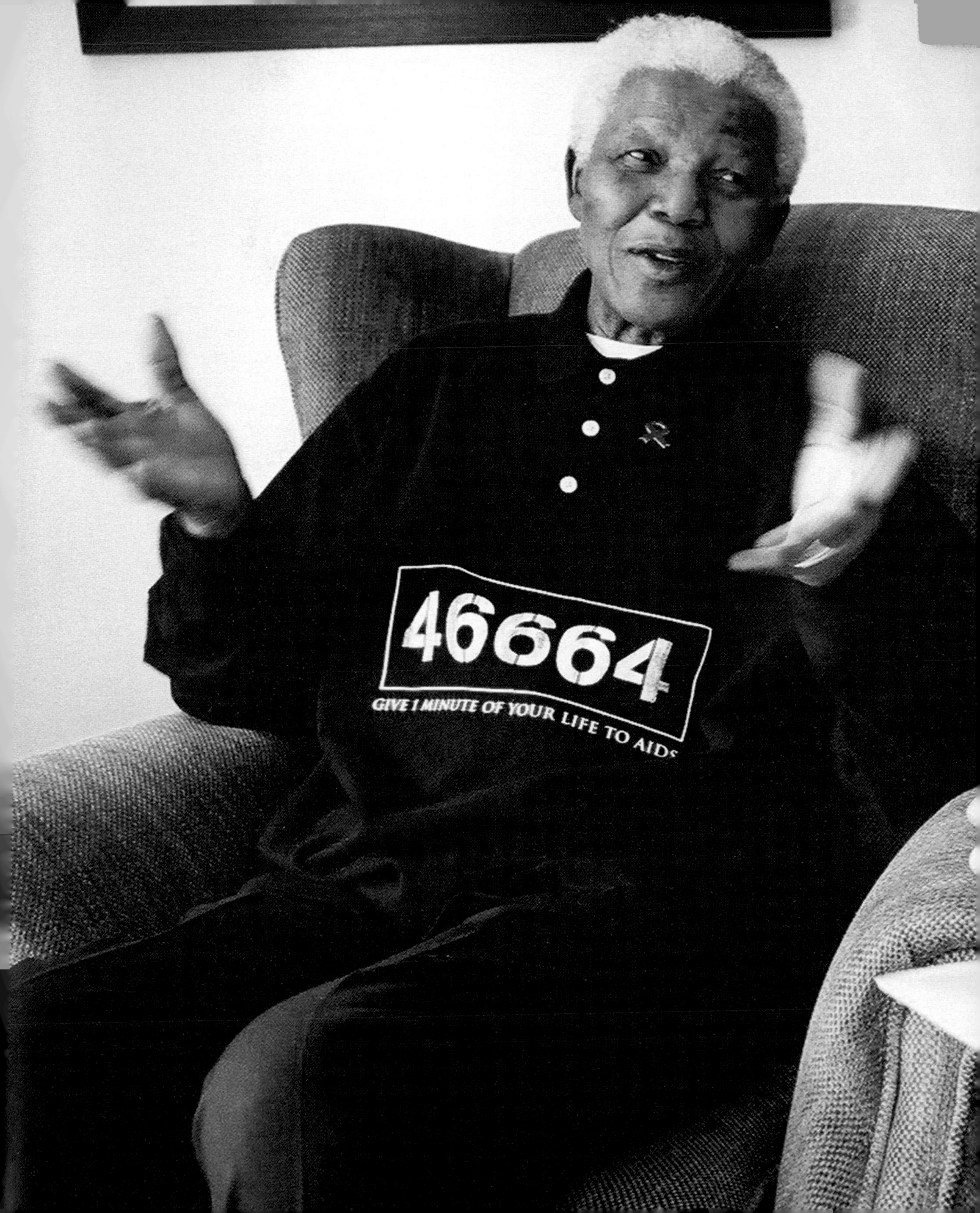
46664
GIVE 1 MINUTE OF YOUR LIFE TO AIDS

Introduction

When Nelson Mandela launched the Nelson Mandela Centre of Memory and Commemoration Project in 2004, he announced his intention to open his prison archive systematically through the Centre. This book documents the first step in that process, and seeks to ensure a wide audience for the stories that have emerged.

Before an investigation by the South African Truth and Reconciliation Commission (TRC) in 1997 and 1998, the official record of Mr Mandela's incarceration remained in the custody of the security establishment, scattered across the departments of Correctional Services and Justice, the South African Police Service and the National Intelligence Agency. Now housed largely in the South African National Archives (following initial interventions by Ahmed Kathrada and urgent recommendations by the TRC), the record remains disorganised, poorly catalogued and difficult to consult. In addition, in terms of the Promotion of Access to Information Act of 2000, only Mr Mandela can authorise access to these files.

Until the establishment of the Centre of Memory, he did this on only one occasion, allowing Anthony Sampson access to the files for the official biography. In order to open up what is now referred to as the Prison Archive, Mr Mandela has now mandated the Centre – in consultation with Ahmed 'Kathy' Kathrada, his confidant and former fellow prisoner, who possesses a passion for history and archives – to manage access to the files. The Centre is systematically documenting the files and working with Kathrada on releasing their contents into the public domain.

The project was launched in 2004 with an exhibition titled 466/64: A Prisoner Working in the Garden, a collaboration with the National Archives that displayed for public viewing a selection of documents from the official archive, along with elements of the Prison Archive from other sources. Many of the latter emerged during, and in response to, the Centre's preparation of the exhibition, and have subsequently been deposited with the Centre.

This book builds on that exhibition to provide a window into the broader Mandela Prison Archive. It offers perspectives on how the official archive came into being and how elements of it have been lost, appropriated and rediscovered. It looks at why the Prison Archive was initiated by prison authorities in the first place, what they wanted to achieve by it and how they tried to make it work. It discovers how their aims were, in part, realised and in other respects subverted.

OPPOSITE:

The incinerator on Robben Island.

BRIEWEBUS
POSTING BOX

LET WEL: BRIEWE WAT BANKNOTE, MUNTSTUKKE, ON-
INGEVULDE POSORDERS OF ANDER ARTIKELS
VAN WAARDE BEVAT, MOET NIE IN HIERDIE
BUS GEPOS WORD NIE. REGISTREER DIT BY
DIE POSKANTOORTOONBANK.

CAUTION: LETTERS CONTAINING BANKNOTES, COINS,
BLANK POSTAL ORDERS OR OTHER
ARTICLES OF VALUE, MUST NOT BE POSTED
IN THIS BOX. REGISTER THEM AT THE POST
OFFICE COUNTER.

Within the official archive, the book shows, it is possible to gain a view of Mr Mandela pursuing his own idea of laying down a record, a project seemingly confounded initially but one that was increasingly successful over time.

Inevitably, the official record has marked emphases, as well as silences, ruptures and contradictions, and an investigation of these is often richly rewarding, yielding even further archival clues and materials. This book explores many of these paths, often leading the reader into parts of the Prison Archive that lie outside the official record, and yet, in many instances, are interweaved with state archives.

A Prisoner in the Garden opens with an account of the Mandela Archive, an infinite source located in innumerable places. The chapter offers a host of archival biographies, and a reading of the stories that became key components of the Prison Archive. Here the reader encounters some of the many attempts to suppress the archive, as well as the struggle to open it up to public scrutiny. The chapter gives substance to what Mr Mandela terms 'the call of justice', the key shaping influence in the creation of the Centre of Memory: unravelling the power relations at play, the drive for secrecy by many powerful interests, and the counter-efforts to attain reasonable access.

Chapter 2 details the records system, the controls over letters and visits, the censorship and obfuscation that underpinned the prison regime. Despite a vast array of regulations and procedures to suppress information about the prisoners, the Prison Archive proved to be irrepressible, this book being but one example of its resilience.

Chapter 3 tells the story of the writing, loss, and return of two of Mr Mandela's prison notebooks, which were 'confiscated' by prison authorities in 1971. The biography of the notebooks, and a following of the archival threads that flow from them, casts a powerful light onto the Prison Archive. It shows us what kind of record Mr Mandela generated, how the prison authorities sought to contain it, and how, in their efforts to exert control, they in turn built up an enormous record of their own, the totality of which comprises the official Prison Archive.

Chapter 4 introduces an array of original texts from the Prison Archive that speak compellingly of the struggle between the prisoners and the authorities for control of the record, and the tactics pursued by each party.

OPPOSITE:

Detail of Robben Island postbox.

The priceless texts reveal how Mr Mandela, in his role as official spokesperson for the prisoners, generated a documentary profusion of his own, engaging the authorities in a dialogue which they tried, with ever-diminishing success, first to ignore and later to resist. At the same time, this archive provides an intimate window into the thoughts and feelings of Nelson Mandela, the man.

Chapter 5 brings the book to a conclusion with the man who walked out of Victor Verster Prison in February 1990 markedly different in appearance from the one who first entered prison in 1962. The prison experience was not only etched on his body, but it permeated his very being. Its role in shaping the future of South Africa remains open to interpretation, but in sharing the Prison Archive with the world, this book invites readers to walk with Mr Mandela on the long road to freedom.

Driven by its founder and the 'call of justice', the Nelson Mandela Foundation, through its Centre of Memory, seeks to tell the stories of a continuing walk to freedom. Mr Mandela exemplifies the understanding that freedom is not something one receives, but rather something that is created. The Centre is premised on a commitment to documenting stories, disseminating information, and contributing to continuing struggles for justice. It is inspired by Mr Mandela and his comrades, who dedicated their lives to these struggles.

The wider Mandela Archive, of which the Prison Archive is a central element, is scattered and bursting with story. For anyone wishing to access the material, the logistical, technical, research and archival challenges are daunting. It is for this very reason that the Centre of Memory identifies and locates sources, and coordinates the endeavours of the many institutions that continue to hold valuable documents and other material, developing a single access point to the many and varied collections. It promotes the idea of an archive for social justice in several ways. It participates in, and often initiates opportunities for, resource sharing, fund-raising and collaborative projects with other institutions, big and small, formal and informal. It engages in, and seeks to stimulate, discussions on the meaning of 'archives for justice', and to challenge secrecy and non-disclosure wherever they threaten democracy and justice. It does this by participating in, or organising, annual conferences, public debates, exhibitions and publications. Through its outreach programmes, as well as study and internship projects, the Centre makes its resources and expertise available to the public, with a special emphasis on reaching disadvantaged communities.

There are three primary dimensions to 'the continuing walk to freedom'. As demonstrated by Mr Mandela himself, humanity can never stop working towards freedom. This is why he has continued to work punishingly hard through his retirement years, and has pursued struggles for justice – in the Burundi peace process, the campaign against HIV/AIDS, the development of rural schools, programmes for children in need, and so on. The Centre documents this continuing walk, and promotes its values.

Mr Mandela has also committed the Centre to making space for the stories that revolve around him. So, for example, the Centre has facilitated (together with the Department of Arts and Culture, the National Cultural History Museum and the Nelson Mandela Museum) the consolidation of his presidential gifts and awards and their formal donation to the state. These are housed in the Nelson Mandela Museum in the city of Mthatha.

In a speech marking the placing of the gifts in the custody of the Museum, Mr Mandela described them as 'honours': honours received on behalf of comrades and colleagues who stood with him in the long struggle for justice, and on behalf of a country whose traditions are steeped in those struggles; honours shared with the country through their public display. The Centre subsequently launched the Izipho: Madiba's Gifts exhibition, a selection of gifts and awards primarily from the post-presidential period. Both exhibitions tell the stories of many thousands of people around the world who have inspired and been inspired by Nelson Mandela.

Finally, the Centre – principally through its exhibitions and publications – actively disseminates these remarkable stories. This book is the first in a series dedicated to ensuring that the archive does not remain within the walls of repositories. At the same time, the Centre, together with a number of institutional partners, has launched a Madiba Legacy Series of comics with a planned initial print run of a million and free distribution. (Madiba is Mr Mandela's clan name by which he is often respectfully addressed.) The comics are designed specifically to overcome resilient systemic barriers to the dissemination of story, particularly those experienced by South Africa's youth. It is our hope that this series will contribute to building a culture of reading in South Africa.

By harnessing Nelson Mandela's legacy, the Centre of Memory carries forward his unique ability to bring people together in dialogue and action shaped by the call of justice. Central to any harnessing of legacy is the concept of memory. Action, if it is to be true to the legacy it claims to represent, must flow from and be shaped by memory. *A Prisoner in the Garden* is a work of memory.

John Samuel
Chief Executive
Nelson Mandela Foundation

OPPOSITE:

Robben Island courtyard, present day.

Since stepping down as President in 1999 Mandela has maintained a full schedule of work.

PRECEDING:

From left to right, Nelson Mandela, Andimba Toivo ja Toivo, Justice Mpanza and unidentified official during media visit to Robben Island in 1977.

OPPOSITE:

From left to right, Frank Anthony, Sandy Sejake and Walter Sisulu in 1977.

ABOVE:

Political prisoners were required to 'garden' during the media visit.

LEFT:

Sedick Isaacs, Robben Island prisoner and librarian.

Photograph of Mandela taken during a visit by journalists to Robben Island in 1977. The caption on the back of the photograph, in Afrikaans, reads: 'A prisoner working in the garden.'

'n Gevangene werksaam in die tuin.

CHAPTER ONE

An Infinite Record
Secrets uncovered and stories retold

On 21 September 2004 Nelson Mandela launched the Nelson Mandela Centre of Memory and Commemoration with the opening, in Johannesburg, of the exhibition 466/64: A Prisoner Working in the Garden, a selection of documents and objects from his long incarceration in apartheid prisons. The title of the exhibition was taken from the official caption to a 1977 photograph of Mandela. The caption is full of irony. Nelson Mandela was not simply 'a prisoner', he was the most famous political prisoner in the world. Neither does the photograph depict him as a 'worker'; instead, the man in the image stands in defiance of arbitrary authority, his body language making a mockery of the spade on which he is leaning. And the 'garden' is not a garden at all. It is a barren strip of land to which some of the prisoners had been herded during the visit to Robben Island by a group of journalists carefully selected by the authorities. The entire scene, in short, was a charade.

There was a garden on Robben Island and Mandela did indeed work in it – a garden made and tended by the prisoners, one that expressed many of the values now firmly associated with Mandela and the comrades who shared his prison experience. The garden – much loved by Mandela – was about 25 metres long and a metre wide, positioned along one side of the courtyard outside the single cells.

The photograph expresses the challenge Nelson Mandela posed to the apartheid system during the years of his incarceration. It also exemplifies the challenge posed – and the richness offered – by all archival records. It is precisely these challenges that this book explores.

The Mandela Archive
The very idea of the Nelson Mandela Centre of Memory and Commemoration suggests a Mandela Archive. But whereas a conventional archive has a single location and a finite number of documents, the Mandela Archive is an infinite one, located in innumerable places. It is also not confined to documents, but includes sites, landscapes, material objects, performances, photographs, artworks, stories and the memories of individuals.

The list is endless, and the full scope of the Mandela Archive is difficult to comprehend. The Mandela Archive is, in the first instance, defined by Mandela himself, and documents his life and work. He is the centre point of the archive, from which a myriad threads can be followed.

One is his childhood in the former Transkei – his own memories, the oral histories recounted by friends and family, various documents of that time, the ruins of his family's homestead at Mvezo, and the rock at Qunu where he used to play as a boy. The family thread leads you to the traditions of his ancestors, and records of three wives, five children and all their offspring. No listing of the Mandela Archive can, however, ever be considered complete or do more than suggest the enormity of its scope and complexity. While some elements may be predictable, like the immense government record of his tenure as president of South Africa, others are entirely unanticipated.

Think, for instance, of that rock at Qunu or the moving poems of Wole Soyinka in the collection *Mandela's Earth*. Although certain parts of the Mandela Archive are but tiny slivers buried in other archives (like the traces of the anti-apartheid and Free Mandela campaigns in the United Nations archive in New York), others are important components of much bigger archives. The Robben Island Museum and the virtual South African History Online are cases in point. Institutions such as the Nelson Mandela Museum and the Robben Island Museum not only hold elements of the Mandela Archive but are, in their entirety, elements of the Mandela Archive in so far as the museums are themselves artefacts – archival traces if you like – of a post-apartheid era hungry for celebrations of the man and his work, and eager to harness his symbolic powers.

The Mandela Archive connects to a host of other archives in powerful ways. While necessarily focusing on Mandela, it also embraces other elements of history of which he has become a symbol. The rural history of the former Transkei is, for example, included in the archival material housed in Mthatha. Mandela's personal history is also that of not only his close comrades, but all who identified with the struggles against apartheid, and is echoed in all the records they generated, in their many and varied forms. Nelson Mandela's story also tells of his interaction with individuals within the police force, as well as the entire security establishment, who repeatedly confronted him, and does this through various records (including graves marked and unmarked) developed to deal with him and others who were seen to threaten state security. The Mandela Archive interlaces in countless ways with the records of the Truth and Reconciliation Commission (TRC). It is central to the intricate web of negotiations between the apartheid government, the African National Congress (ANC) and the various other political parties, which led to the first democratic elections in South Africa. It includes records of South Africa's intensive diplomatic and foreign engagement with and around Mandela, as well as those related to conflict resolution across the globe. And much more besides.

OPPOSITE:

The 'sliding rock' at Qunu in the Eastern Cape on which Mandela played as a boy.

Viewing Another Archive

The helicopter drops out of a cloudless winter sky at Mvezo in the Eastern Cape. Nelson Mandela has arrived at his birthplace on his 87th birthday. With him are his wife Graça Machel, and Jakes Gerwel – Director General during Mandela's presidency and now Chairperson of the Nelson Mandela Foundation – and a few members of staff.

For days the world's media have been trying to find out what he will be doing on his birthday. They have not been told that he wishes to visit Mvezo again, and to share the moment with Gerwel. Mvezo is not only Mandela's birthplace, but also a satellite (along with Qunu and Mthatha) of the three-part Nelson Mandela Museum, and thus an important component of the broader archive.

The staff set up a picnic table and chairs on a platform set centrally in the ruins of the homestead where Mandela's father, chief of Mvezo, had resided. The ruins spill across the edge of a ridge, the village of Mvezo not visible about half a kilometre further back on the ridge, and before the viewer a majestic landscape of a U-shaped river valley reaches up into a range of mountains. Just across the mountains is the village of Idutywa, birthplace of fellow Robben Islander Govan Mbeki and his son Thabo, who succeeded Mandela as president of a democratic South Africa.

Mandela wears dark glasses and a sun hat. From a distance he looks remarkably like the 1977 'prisoner in the garden'. He points at the ruins of one of several huts that made up the homestead: 'That is my place of birth.' His right hand holds a glass of champagne. Not ten metres from where he sits is an ancient grinding stone. 'That is where my mother would grind maize. She was an excellent grinder.'

The old man is relaxed, happy. The stories are beginning to come. But the local villagers have gathered to the sound of the landing helicopter, and now pour down the hill and into the ruins of the homestead. Madiba watches them arrive with a smile. 'Ah, very good,' he says. He insists on being introduced to all the children, nearly a hundred of them. Then to the elders. Finally, he sits for almost half an hour with the current chief of Mvezo. They discuss community matters, catch up on family histories.

It is time to leave. Mandela pulls out his wallet and carefully counts out the money for a cow, a gift to the community.

The Mandela Archive incorporates, among a vast number of other elements, the following:

- The personal memories of Mandela, as communicated orally by himself.
- Oral accounts of the histories and traditions of both his family and his clan.
- The actual prison cells in which he was incarcerated – Marshall Square, Newlands Jail, the Old Fort, Pretoria Central Prison, Robben Island, Pollsmoor, and the prison house at Victor Verster.
- Other historic sites where he has left his trace.
- Artefacts used by him or given to him. Three institutions, for example, hold collections of gifts and awards – the Nelson Mandela Museum, the African National Congress and the Nelson Mandela Foundation.
- The records of the Robben Island General Recreational Committee, a formally constituted prisoners' committee.
- The oral histories of friends, comrades, associates and employees of Mandela.
- The ever-shifting contents of innumerable websites.
- Mandela's own writings and speeches.
- His personal notes, diaries and other papers.
- Documents of births, marriages, deaths, divorces and education.
- The official records of Mandela's trials and imprisonments.
- Letters from him to others, and their responses.
- Medical records.
- The documents generated by him as a lawyer, as well as those drawn up by the many lawyers who have acted on his behalf.
- The official record of his tenure as president of South Africa.
- Foreign government records.
- The records of the African National Congress.
- The Truth and Reconciliation Commission.
- Media reports in print, sound and visual forms.
- The records of fraternal political organisations around the world, notably those associated with the Anti-Apartheid Movement.
- Scholarly discourse on his life and work, found in books, articles, conference papers, and so on.
- Wherever he figures in poetry, song and graphic art.
- The many structures, from bridges and schools to statues and streets, named after him.
- The archives of the organisations founded by him, notably the Nelson Mandela Foundation, the Nelson Mandela Childrens' Fund and The Mandela Rhodes Foundation.
- The countless stories of people who have simply felt their lives touched by him.

STOP APARTHEID NOW!

TRÓCAIRE

FREE

ANC

MANDELA

Sign up for Democracy

ANC Signature Campaign

Demand a Constituent Assembly and an Interim Government NOW!

No to Apartheid No to Dictatorship Nov. 2

PEP

NOW FREE ALL SOUTH AFRICAN POLITICAL PRISONERS

MANDELA RELEASED!

FREE South Africa NOW!

RELEASE MANDELA CAMPAIGN
"The People Shall Govern"

I MUST RETURN

Nelson MANDELA

un doctorado a la dignidad humana

Solidaridad con el Pueblo Sudafricano

UNIVERSIDAD DE CARABOBO

RELEASE MANDELA

& all political prisoners

STOP APARTHEID'S VIOLENCE

Over 5,000 People Have Been Killed Since Nelson Mandela's Release. You Can Help Stop It!

For More Information Contact
THE AFRICA FUND
198 Broadway
New York, N.Y. 10038
(212) 962-1210

HAPPY BIRTHDAY
NELSON MANDELA

A PEOPLE'S LEADER
FREEDOM AT 70

Release Nelson Mandela
and all political prisoners of South Africa and Namibia!

Anti-Apartheid Movement 13 Mandela St London NW1 0DW 01-387 7966

Mandela
kom huis toe

Na 27 jaar in gevangenis

LEES RAAKWYS

Uitgereik deur Raakwys Editorial Collective

NELSON MANDELA

"I have fought against white domination and I have fought against black domination. I have cherished the ideal of a democratic and free society in which all persons live together in harmony and with equal opportunities. It is an ideal which I hope to live for and to achieve. But if needs be, it is an ideal for which I am prepared to die."

UP BEAT

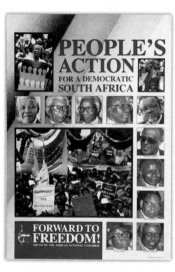

PEOPLE'S
ACTION
FOR A DEMOCRATIC
SOUTH AFRICA

SUPPORT
THE
RESTRICTED

FORWARD TO
FREEDOM!
ISSUED BY THE AFRICAN NATIONAL CONGRESS

MANDELA
RELEASED!

ANC

FREE ALL
POLITICAL PRISONERS!

LAUDIUM
WELCOMES

COMRADE
MANDELA

MANDELA FOR
PRESIDENT

ANC

THE PEOPLE'S CHOICE!

Personal

With the establishment of the Centre of Memory, Mandela himself was motivated to unearth two crates of
his personal papers (including items that predate his incarceration) and to deposit them with the Centre.
His Methodist Church membership cards of 1929—1934 are, for example, among the items that – quite
astonishingly – survived the various depredations that struck the Mandela home in his long absence.
The crates also contained his diaries and desk calendars for the period 1976—1998, a number of his
notebooks and certain prison documents, as well as the private notes he made during the negotiations of
Codesa (Convention for a Democratic South Africa, the first formal forum for the transfer of power),
a remarkable counterpoint to the official Codesa record in the National Archives.

Safely Lodged

Certain records – such as those held in the National Archives of South Africa and the National Archives of
the United Kingdom (documents of the Commonwealth Relations Office, the Foreign and Commonwealth
Office and the Foreign Office) – are safely lodged in official repositories, although many may require
professional assistance to unearth. Some are better secured than others, and some remain undisclosed,
and hence unknown, in the secret files of foreign intelligence agencies.

Inadvertently Secret

Some records remain inadvertently secret, simply because they have gone astray, while others form
incidental components of larger archives. Mandela's divorce papers, for example, can be found in court
records; material relevant to his career as a lawyer lies with the Department of Justice; and a file on his
former attorney, Ismail Ayob, can be found in the International Defence and Aid Collection at the Mayibuye
Archives (University of the Western Cape / Robben Island Museum).

Fugitive

Some of the archives were fugitive: like the Mandela memoirs written in secret on Robben Island and
smuggled abroad; the sparse record of the ANC underground; the 1980s People's History Trust collection,
which documented the South African struggle from a base in Zimbabwe; and the records of the ANC in exile.
While many of these have been drawn into safe custody and placed in the public domain, others have not.

Lost and Found

Many records have been appropriated, some secreted away from their original holding places, others sold or lost; of these, numbers are slowly returning.

Dormant

Still other records – notably personal testimonies – lie dormant, awaiting chance discovery or some other opportune moment to emerge. The Robben Island Memories Project, which collects the personal testimonies of ex-political prisoners and conducts interviews with their families and with warders, draws out such records. Individuals close to Mandela hold records of their interactions with him, awaiting the right opportunity for release.

Operational

The records of Mandela's presidency from 1994 to 1999 are still operational and remain with the government structures concerned, such as the Cabinet and Presidential archives, and in numerous government departments. The same holds true for the records of his personal office since 1999.

Consigned and Recalled

Parts of the Mandela Archive were consigned to dusty files and emerged only with the establishment of the Centre of Memory. In 2004 Himan Bernadt, of the legal firm Bernadt, Vukic, Potash & Getz, presented the Centre with the firm's collection of legal files on Nelson Mandela covering the period 1966–1990. Journalist Sahm Venter amassed a collection of some 120 tapes of press conferences, speeches and interviews from the period leading up to Mandela's release, the immediate aftermath and into the presidential years. A digital copy of these tapes is now lodged with the Centre. The Nelson Mandela Foundation itself, and its two sister foundations – the Nelson Mandela's Children Fund and The Mandela Rhodes Foundation – have similarly come to recognise the extent of the Mandela Archive present in all their work.

Letter of gratitude from
Mandela to his lawyer.

The Bernadt Collection

Many lawyers attended to Nelson Mandela's legal and related matters during his incarceration. The Cape Town-based legal firm Bernadt, Vukic, Potash & Getz (formerly Frank, Bernadt & Joffe) coordinated the work in the period 1966–1990. In 2004 Himan Bernadt presented the Centre of Memory with the firm's legal files on Mandela.

Repeatedly, Mandela resorted to the threat of legal action where the authorities broke or failed to follow their own rules, and the firm's files document Mandela's determination to challenge the system using every means available to him.

G 300(a)

Copy.

BESOEK VAN REGSADVISEUR
LEGAL ADVISER'S VISIT

VERLOFBRIEF VIR BESOEK AAN n GEVANGENE / PERMIT TO VISIT A
PRISONER

S. E. Kahlahn and

Ek, die ondergetekende
I, the undersigned .... W. J. Kugnonen ....
(Drukskrif/Print)

Verklaar dat my besoek aan gevangene no. ...466/66......
State that my visit to prisoner no.

Naam
Name ..... Nelson Mandela ....

Vir die onderstaande regsake afgelê word, naamlik ..in Connexion with..
Is for the following legal business, viz

..Seizure of Records at his motta ....

....

Ek is te volle vertroud met die bepali s van Artikel 47(a) van die
WET OP GEVANGENISSE,
I hereby pledge that my visit to the said prisoner will be confined
strictly to the said legal business, that I am fully conversant

1959 (WET NO. 8 1959) soos gewysig en die bepalings van Regulasie
123(4)(a) en (b) van die GEKONSOLIDEERDE GEVANGENISREGULASIES

with the provisions of section 47 of the PRISONS ACT, 1959
(ACT 8 of 1959) as amended and ion 123(4)(a) and (b)
of the CONSOLIDATED PRISONS REGULATIONS made in terms of section
uitgeva rdig kragtens Wet 8 van 1959 soos gewysig. Ek beloof hiermee
dat my besoek aan genoemde gevangene streng by die bespreking
van die gemelde regsake bepaal sal word en dat ek geen ander onder=
werpe sal aanroer of as bemiddelaar tussen genoemde gevangene en
enige ander persoon of omgekeer sal optree nie, nog iets wat

ninety-four of the PRISONS ACT, 1959 (Act. No. 8 of 1959) as
amended; and that I will not discuss any other matter with
the prisoner or serve as an intermediary between the said prisoner
ek te wete mag kom terwyl ek in die gevangenis is openbaar
sal maak sonder om nie eers van die veran twoordelike owerhede
verlof daartoe te verkry nie.

and any other person or vice versa, nor will I divulge anything
that may come to my knowledge whilst in the Prison without having
first obtained permission to do so from the proper authorities.

....18/4/177......
REGSVERTEENWOORDIGER/LEGA ADVISER   Datum/Date

....
HOOF VAN GEVANGENIS/HEAD OF THE   Datum/Date
PRISON

The files also demonstrate Mandela's use of the legal arena to engage the world outside prison. He used his lawyers to look after the interests of his family. In particular, they sought to protect Winnie from continuing harassment by the state. In 1966, he successfully resisted attempts by the Transvaal Law Society to have him struck off the roll of practising attorneys. The following year, together with fellow-prisoner Wilton Mkwayi, he appealed successfully against his listing by the state as a 'Communist'. And his lawyers became an effective conduit for the literature Mandela craved.

Convention for a Democratic South Africa

Having initiated negotiations with the apartheid state from his prison cell in the 1980s, the period following Nelson Mandela's release (1990–1994) was one of intense continuing negotiation between the African National Congress and the state. As president of the ANC, Mandela was at the hub of this process. Using diaries, notebooks and files, he meticulously documented his involvement. Record-keeping habits cultivated during the long years of his incarceration are clearly evident in the resultant archive. Two files from his personal collection, for example, cover the proceedings of the Convention for a Democratic South Africa (Codesa), which opened the formal negotiations between all South Africa's political groupings, as well as related negotiation processes. The files contain a rich collection of precisely the kinds of record that usually escape any professional archiving process – draft speeches, notes, discussion points and messages sent to and received from colleagues. As with the Prison Archive, they provide a rich and intimate window into the thinking of an individual and his organisation during a critical period in South Africa's history.

1.

Share developments in democratic process

2.

Our problem is to face the very 1st democratic elections with 17 million voters who have never voted before.

3.

Illiteracy rate of 67% and 63% of our voters are rural based.

4.

Our problem is how to access people and introduce voters to education on how to vote.

5.

We are contesting this election with the NP. which has already 150 election offices. We have none save our 14 regional offices.

6

NP is one of the most efficient & well-organised political parties in country.

7

Enjoy massive support. Opinion polls indicate that we would emerge as majority party. But clearest thing is to be able to carry voters to voting booth.

8

Nelson Mandela
by.
by Jacques Derrida
&
Mustapha Tlili

C·O·D·E·S·A

Public Media Observations on Codesa

End of first day of Codesa shallowed atmosphere of bonhomie that had been created and marked the start of "real" negotiations.

Codesa will survive battle. But last night's battle showed that the Govt is going to fight hard and close to dirty — and the Anc will lash out equally viciously if it feels it is being like a pricannin. Govt put Anc on the spot with its out-of-the-blue proposal for far-reaching short-term changes to the structure of Parliament and the executive use — Star editorial 21/12/91

∧ ∧ ∧

The IFP is raising quibbles at every available opportunity.

Codesa was even prepared to offer the King an opportunity to address the meeting

It is fair to entertain that the party might be seeking to raise its profile in the multi party process by raising unnecessary objections. It is fair to say that people

CONVENTION FOR A DEMOCRATIC SOUTH AFRICA

LISSADELL

Cde Cheryl   9. 11. 93

The Deputy-President and Cde Stofile have agreed to go to Umtata tomorrow. Do you think you could leave Graeme again Just for one day?

Tata

The deputy President & Cde Stofile have discussed it with me. We have agreed to go to Umtata tomorrow. I'm not too keen on leaving Graeme! (It's ok).

Cheryl

Archival secrecy and the operation of power

A major part of the Mandela Archive is inevitably embedded in the record of the apartheid state. And this, unavoidably, means having to deal with the secrecy surrounding certain components and even the loss of some archival records. Mandela's personal notebooks (see Chapter 3) are but one instance in which the state's record was, and in some instances continues to be, compromised. Under apartheid, a multitude of laws, procedures and practices kept 'sensitive' materials out of the public domain or closely monitored access to them. This continued even after the first democratic elections and the lifting of much of apartheid's repressive apparatus. Mandela's archive – and, most particularly, his Prison Archive – as well as a host of interlaced records, remained out of public reach.

Under apartheid the records of the state were governed by the 1962 Archives Act, which determined that government records with archival value should be transferred to the State Archives Service (precursor to the National Archives) after 30 years. Yet another provision of the Act allowed records in the custody of the Service to be opened to public scrutiny when they reached 30 years of age. In other words, public access was, in principle, limited only by the 30-year 'closed period'. The 1996 National Archives of South Africa Act reduced the closed period to 20 years.

During the apartheid era the State Archives Service was unable or unwilling to bring the security establishment under its control, with the result that in 1994 most of the state's files on Mandela remained in the sole custody of security agencies. It took the intervention of Ahmed Kathrada and then the Truth and Reconciliation Commission (TRC) to have this amended. In 1997 and 1998 a TRC investigative team audited surviving security records, and documented the systematic destruction of state records between 1990 and 1994. In 1991 the National Intelligence Service had, for example, initiated a wide-ranging disposal exercise that extended across the security establishment. Using the logbook of a truck carrying documents bound for an Iscor furnace, the TRC team calculated that in three months of 1993 alone some 44 tons of documents originating from the National Intelligence Service were destroyed!

The destruction was not confined to the security establishment itself, but extended to other departments. In the run-up to the transfer of power, and in a move approved by Cabinet, all government departments were advised by the Security Secretariat to destroy every classified document received from other sources, especially documents relating to the National Security Management System.

ABOVE:

The Iscor facility in Pretoria viewed from the Voortrekker Monument, where National Intelligence Service records were destroyed.

While a moratorium on the destruction of state records had already been mooted by the ANC Commission on Museums, Monuments and Heraldry in 1992, it was only in November 1995 – more than a year after the transfer of power to a democratically elected government – that the new Cabinet approved a moratorium on the destruction of all records of state. It was a moratorium announced by Mandela himself, and remained in force until the work of the TRC had been completed. Despite this, the National Intelligence Service (later the National Intelligence Agency) continued with the systematic destruction of documents until late into 1996.

The TRC investigative team lobbied for the surviving records of the security establishment to be transferred to the National Archives. In the years that followed, a steady trickle of State Security Council, Police, Justice and Correctional Services records were deposited with the National Archives. The record is, however, patchy. In Mandela's case, material that remains unaccounted for includes items confiscated from him during arrests and raids and not used in evidence in trials, as well as documents from the files of both the Security Police and National Intelligence. And the evidence suggests that the official prison record on Mandela, extensive as it is, has also been depleted. Former warder Christo Brand, for instance, reports that a Robben Island photographic record of Mandela and a Pollsmoor prison incident book have disappeared.

While a loophole in the current legislation continues to allow military and National Intelligence records to remain with the creating agencies, the assumption was that the transferred files would become subject to the new 20-year rule in terms of public access. However, in 2000 Parliament passed the Promotion of Access to Information Act, which overrides any other legislation on public access. The act determines that personal information be protected until 20 years after an individual's death. The challenge to archival secrecy is thus tempered by the right to privacy. Power is at play in all of these concepts and in the tension between them.

Opening the Mandela Archive is an effort towards making the record available to the public. At the same time, the Centre of Memory also needs to take into account the legacy of the security establishment and its surveillance programme, which intruded into the private worlds of activists like Mandela, subjecting their most intimate emotions and actions to invasive scrutiny. To do this, the Centre enters the fraught domain of choosing to open up some documents to the public while leaving others to enjoy a new privacy. It does so in the knowledge that every such act is not simply a gesture of sensitivity, but also an act of power, albeit a retrieval of power for those once so actively disempowered. No archival act, it seems, is ever innocent of power.

OPPOSITE:
The private in the public: divorce order of Mandela and his first wife Evelyn.

U.D.J. 611.

FINAL ORDER OF DIVORCE.
IN THE SUPREME COURT OF SOUTH AFRICA,
~~WITWATERSRAND LOCAL DIVISION~~ DIVISION.

At **JOHANNESBURG**, on the **19th** day of **MARCH**, 195**8**.

Before the Honourable Mr. Justice **WILLIAMSON.**

In the matter between

NELSON MANDELA, Plaintiff,

and

EVELYN MANDELA, born MASE, Defendant.

Having heard Mr. **A.P. O'DOWD,**

counsel for the Plaintiff, and having read the documents filed of record

IT IS ORDERED

1. That the bonds of marriage subsisting between Plaintiff and Defendant be and are hereby dissolved.

2. **That the Agreement between the Parties filed of record, and marked 'B' be and is hereby made an Order of Court.**

BY ORDER OF THE COURT.

_____

Asst *Registrar.*

NOTE.—Indicate whether order has been made in terms of section 1 (1) (a) of Act No. 32 of 1935: Yes/No.

Archival secrecy is thus by no means the preserve of oppressive regimes. One particular example illustrates this well. In 1964 the president of the ANC, Albert Luthuli, wrote a letter to the United Nations, calling on that body to put pressure on the apartheid regime not to hand down the death sentence to Mandela and his fellow Rivonia trialists. The Centre requested access to the letter in 2005, and was told by the UN that the letter is classified and would have to go through a lengthy declassification process before it could be made available. The record of the TRC – supposedly a record of public expiation of guilt – itself was also deemed sensitive and placed under a veil of secrecy, despite the Commission's own recommendations that its records be transferred to the National Archives and be as available as possible for public consultation through nationwide centres of memory, for example. New security systems at the National Archives have, however, built a wall around the TRC records, and researchers continue to report difficulties in securing ready access to material. An undocumented volume of TRC records was removed by commissioners and staffers when the Commission closed. And, in a protracted and expensive court action, the South African History Archive ultimately succeeded in forcing the transfer of 34 boxes of 'sensitive' TRC files from the Ministry of Intelligence to the National Archives and securing public access to over half of them. In many ways, the record of the TRC has come to exemplify the space democracy provides for contesting access to information.

The TRC was itself archive, an archive set up to be consulted, confronted, engaged. It exemplifies the notion of archives for social justice, having moved away from the 19th-century record of colonial information for, and practices of, domination in which the official South African archival system originated. It is archive moulded by the experiences of the 20th century and especially the complexity of the struggle against apartheid – an archive that is highly desirable but also easily jeopardised.

Records in jeopardy

It is precisely the high profile of Mandela that enables the Centre to draw attention to records that are endangered or might otherwise be neglected. Even where the official record has not been actively suppressed, it has often been found to be at risk.

In 1994, in terms of the 30-year rule, the Department of Justice transferred to the State Archives Service the official record of the Rivonia Trial. To the horror of the Service, the record consisted of only fragments and, for the next two years, the Service embarked on a thorough investigation into the loss of the great bulk of this record. The result was inconclusive, and to this day the missing material has not been found.

During its investigation, the Service identified a substantial collection of Rivonia records at the University of the Witwatersrand – materials donated by the defence lawyers – and a small microfilm collection at the University of Cape Town. The Service also discovered that prosecutor Percy Yutar had in his possession a significant collection of prosecution records that constitute part of the official record. Yutar, however, argued that the records he had retained were working copies, taken purely for consultation at home. While negotiating with him over the status of these documents, the Service discovered that he had sold his collection to Harry Oppenheimer, a wealthy collector of Africana, who had then placed them in the Brenthurst Library located on his private estate in Johannesburg. What followed was a vigorous, and often bitter, public debate concerning the future of the documents. Eventually Mandela intervened personally, seeking a compromise. He secured for the State Archives Service hard and microform copies of the records held at Brenthurst.

The tale of the dispersed official record of the Rivonia Trial had at least two further twists. Firstly, it was revealed after Yutar's death that he had not sold everything to Oppenheimer. In 2001, his son put a number of documents up for auction in London, where they were bought by South African businessman Douw Steyn. They remain in Steyn's possession. Secondly, when in April 2005 the Centre of Memory examined the Yutar collection at Brenthurst, it discovered that only about half the collection had been copied for the National Archives. The richest material – mainly documents confiscated by the police at Lilliesleaf farm (where most of the Rivonia trialists were arrested) and used as evidence in the trial (including handwritten notes by Mandela, as well as his diary) – had not been copied. The Centre of Memory is now working closely with the Brenthurst Library to ensure that this priceless archival resource is placed in the public domain effectively.

OVERLEAF:

Rivonia Trial records in private possesion, purchased at an auction in London. Documents have been autographed by various people since the purchase.

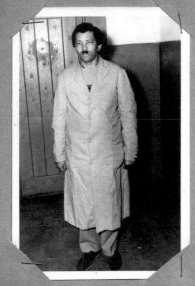

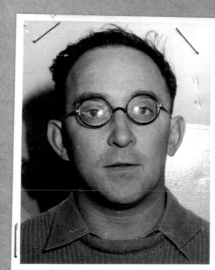

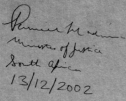

Seeing and touching these historic
documents so many decades after the
Rivonia Trial evoke an inexplicable
emotion in one, especially on the day
when Dow [turns] fifty! Happy
Birthday Dow. I wish you fifty more and
happier returns, Master Dow.

[signature]
Minister of Justice
South Africa
13/12/2002

A valuable collection only a
Douw Steyn can assemble.

NMandela
26. 6. 03

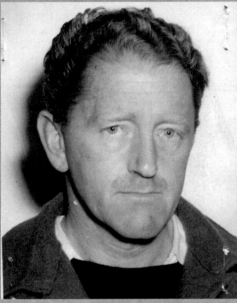

Douw —

This is a priceless piece
of the history of liberty.
I give you credit.

Bill Clinton
19 - May - 03

This is the greatest contribution you have
made to the history of this country. You
only make our struggle worth while. It
is people like yourself Douw whose
unsung heroism will go down in
history as having made South Africa
what it is to-day.

Long after we are gone, sustain the
democracy our children died for. Their
blood was not spilt in vain.

Amandla!!
Power to all the people of South Africa

Winnie Mandela
23. 8. 2004

But documents have not only evaded the boundaries of the official repository; many remain adrift within the archives system itself. The post-1994 government decided to consolidate all the official prison records of political prisoners and to place them in the custody of the National Archives in Pretoria. For some reason, certain Robben Island records – including files on Mandela – were instead handed over to the Cape Archives Repository in Cape Town. This repository, providing public access according to the 20-year rule, allowed a researcher to copy parts of the collection and, in early 2005, a journalist used this material to prepare an article, drawing the attention of the Centre to the archive. The Centre intervened, briefing the National Archivist and recommending that the material be transferred to Pretoria. This has been agreed to in principle by the National Archivist.

In some cases, valuable records are in physical danger – quite literally. The official archive relating to the Madiba clan and its role in the history of the Eastern Cape, as well as that of the many chiefdoms of the region, is for example an astonishingly rich resource for South African history. Constructed by successive colonial and later segregationist and apartheid bureaucracies seeking knowledge of the African populations whom they sought to rule, the historical record we now have – biased as it was in terms of the recording of information deemed to be important for administration and, indeed, for domination – was nonetheless a sustained and systematic recording effort. Read with a sensitivity as to the circumstances under which it was compiled, it is a record rich in material pertinent to the history of the local African population, both because of the extent to which it laid down elements of precolonial epistemologies, and for the light it casts on the tumultuous transition from a pre-industrial order to a modern one, in the context of emerging segregation. It is, however, a record in danger.

Under apartheid what was the Transkei homeland established its own state archives service. The 'independence' of this institution – as in many other spheres – was bolstered by the fact that the South African government of the time considered it a full-fledged national archives. Although the Transkei Archives was desperately under-resourced, colonial- and apartheid-era collections in Cape Town were transferred to the Transkeian capital, Umtata (today Mthatha), where they were stored in the central administrative building, the Bhunga Building, in relatively good condition. After 1994, the Transkei Archives was absorbed into the new Eastern Cape Provincial Archives Service, which decided to maintain depots in Mthatha, Port Elizabeth and King William's Town. In the latter two locations, excellent archival facilities were secured. In 2000 the Bhunga Building became the site of the Nelson Mandela Museum, under the aegis of what was then the national Department of Arts, Culture, Science and Technology.

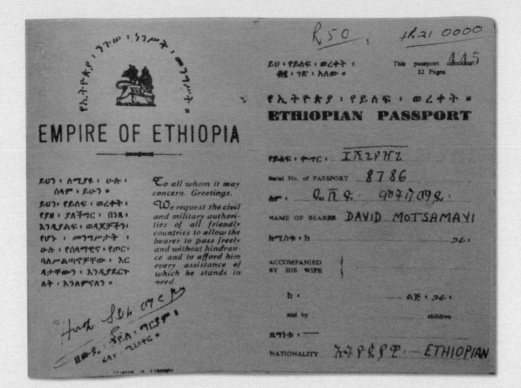

Documents used as evidence against Mandela at the Rivonia Trial.

ABOVE:

Mandela's Ethiopian passport, using the alias David Motsamayi.

LEFT:

A page from Mandela's 1962 diary.

The museum, however, decided to relocate the Transkei Archives, but when the provincial government was unable to secure alternative accommodation, the material was simply placed in a storeroom in the backyard. The conditions were appalling, with nonexistent security, a leaking roof, broken windows and no climatic or fire control. Records were damaged, and the two members of staff struggled to provide any meaningful professional service. Over nearly three years the National Archives mediated between the provincial government and the museum, but no satisfactory solution has yet been found. The storeroom's facilities have been improved significantly, but the situation remains one of serious concern.

The reimagining of South Africa

In convening the Mandela Archive, the Centre enters a dialogue with current custodians – librarians, friends, comrades, thieves, perpetrators, journalists, lawyers and many others – in order to encourage them to preserve these records for posterity, to explore their content and to reveal their secrets.

Acute resource shortages, however, dog almost all official archival repositories in the country. This is allied to – and, in part, flows from – limited recognition among politicians and state officials of the potential of these and other archives in helping South Africans rediscover who they are, and recreate their own identities. In many instances such identity projects remain prisoner to the constraints and limitations of the official archive as a product of the colonial and apartheid era. Few archival professionals have the requisite skills to rethink the apartheid archival legacy, and to inaugurate policies and projects that challenge or reshape it. The Centre of Memory is an opportunity to confront this challenge and to develop conditions conducive to meeting it.

OPPOSITE AND OVERLEAF:
Documents used as evidence in the Rivonia Trial, now privately owned. These include plans and photographs of Lilliesleaf farm.

All state archives are primarily concerned with preserving the record of government, but, as an arm of government, are vulnerable to political pressures from those in power to safeguard their interests, sometimes at the expense of the public good. Grounding the Mandela Archive in a private foundation asserts its significance – and that of archives in general – to the public good. As such it becomes the focus for the energies of wider 'archives for justice' movements. It is the vehicle, in short, for a centring of energies, memories and stories.

nly now they become more frequent. Like …
wrong, fury, frustration and contempt for what Whites do.

BLACK, COLOURED AND ASIAN ARE SICK TO DEATH OF WHITE SUPREMACY

Sabotage erupts every other week throughout the country, now here, now there. The White are turning vicious and
Already we see the sinister birth-pangs of the lynch gang, the vigilante and the O.A.S. - armed Whites - only
protection" groups, women's pistol clubs, a proliferation of neo-Nazi secret societies. At this rate, within a year
South Africa will be embroiled in the second - bloodier, more furious - Algerian war.

WHILE APARTHEID LEADS TO WAR,

THE GOVERNMENT STOKES THE FIRES

All Verwoerd can do is tighten oppression. He doesn't dare relax. The Army build-up, police re-organisation, the
Branch, arms factories and the Sabotage Act are supposed to make you safe. Yet the harder the Government tries
e resistance to apartheid, the stronger, more determined it has become. Despite Vorster's promised death penalty,

SABOTAGE AND MURDERS MULTIPLIED LAST YEAR

Vorster's Threats Deter Nobody.

...OTAGE AND MURDER WILL NOT CEASE, because:: /

…shift people wholesale as if they were livestock
…cessive Governments have armed the Whites with every power to restrict other people and force them to move - influx
…trol, the Western Cape Removal scheme, banishments and now the "ease race friction" Bill The result - broken homes,
… whole families condemned to starvation in the reserves.

…ou jail a whole people for passes.
…ly Africans must carry passes In 1961, according to Vorster, 375,417 Africans were convicted for pass offences. Po-
…e said they were lenient.

…ou pay hunger wages.
… 1961, the average yearly income of Whites in private construction jobs, for instance, was R1939. If you were Black,
…u got R362. Do you think anyone can raise a family and live a full life on that?

O YOU THINK YOU CAN TREAT MEN LIKE THIS AND GET AWAY WITH IT?

White rule means baasskap and, in the end, domination depends on massacre. Who do you think you're fooling
when you talk about "seperate rights in your own seperate areas" or "White leadership with justice"? Sharpeville after
Sharpeville, the White men ruling this country have killed when they felt their hegemony threatened.

VIOLENCE BREEDS VIOLENCE IN RETURN

You now face an indefinitely long future of terror, uncertainty and steadily eroding power. You will keep a gun
at your side, not knowing whom to trust. Perhaps the street-cleaner is a saboteur, perhaps the man who makes you tea at
the office has a gun. You will never be safe and you will never be sure Because White power - industry, arms, police
- depends on Non-White labour.

YOU WILL HAVE LAUNCHED A WAR YOU CANNOT WIN

APARTHEID IS THE KILLER

SCRAP APARTHEID

APARTHEID — FEAR, HATE, WAR

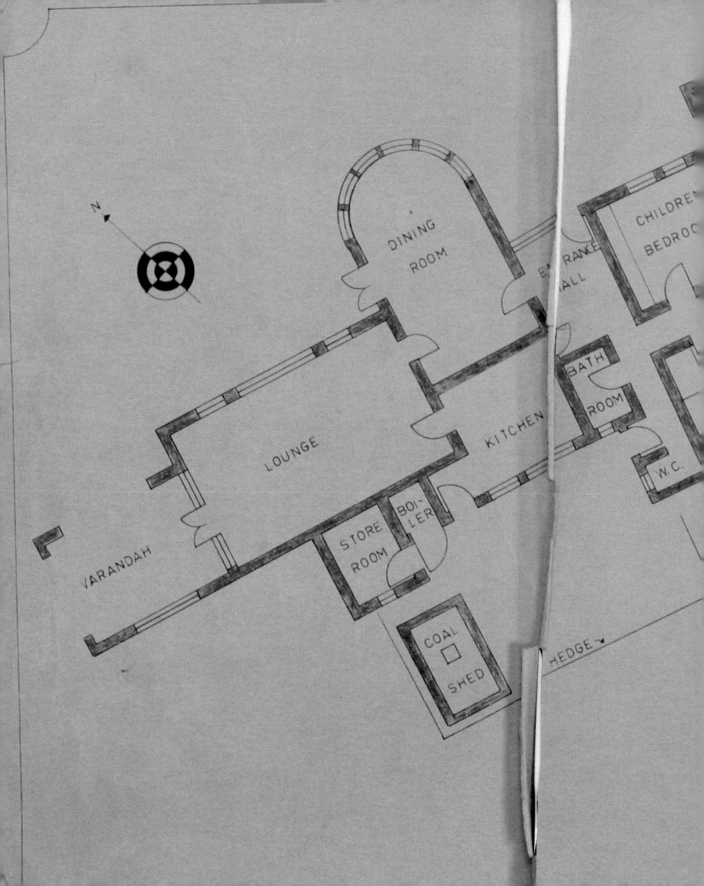

N

DINING ROOM

CHILDREN BEDROOM

ENTRANCE HALL

BATH ROOM

LOUNGE

KITCHEN

W.C.

VARANDAH

BOI-LER

STORE ROOM

COAL SHED

HEDGE

MAIN BEDROOM

BATH ROOM

STUDIO

CHILDREN PLAYROOM

HEDGE

064

CHAPTER TWO

The Prison Archive

More than a simple story of an unjust incarceration

The story of Mandela's life and work has been endlessly told and retold: in secret by freedom fighters to shore up their courage and to mobilise their comrades; in the press in countless attempts to inform, or manipulate, the public; in the collection of his writings and statements from the dock before his incarceration in 1964 (published as *No Easy Walk to Freedom* in 1965); in various memoirs and biographies of him and of others; in the autobiography, *Long Walk to Freedom*; and in numerous academic studies. The main points are well known, and finer detail is available in many accounts. Nonetheless, the Prison Archive offers a novel window into the incarceration years, opening up new views on Mandela the man, on the procedures and practices of prison, on the entanglement of the personal and the collective, on the workings of power and on the nature of archives themselves.

The opening of Mandela's Prison Archive involves much more than the telling of the stories of an unjust incarceration. To open the Prison Archive is to reverse acts of confinement and to make visible those the system rendered invisible. Just as the documents of the prison authorities testify to the effort they put into maintaining a rigidly disciplined and coercive system, so too the documents of the prisoners themselves are testimony to how they challenged that power. One such example is the archive of the Robben Island General Recreational Committee, which documents not only the day-to-day lives of those prisoners held in communal cells, but also how they turned the challenges of the prison system into opportunities for themselves.

Mandela served two terms as a sentenced prisoner and a number of spells in detention or awaiting trial. In June 1952 he experienced his first taste of incarceration when, as a consequence of the civil disobedience protest that came to be known as the Defiance Campaign, he spent two days in Marshall Square police station in Johannesburg. Less than a month later he was charged with violating the Suppression of Communism Act, and arrested along with 19 other leaders of the Defiance Campaign. For this he received a suspended sentence. In December 1956 Mandela and another 155 leaders were charged with treason, and held in another Johannesburg jail, the Old Fort, for several weeks until they were charged.

OPPOSITE:

The Old Fort prison in Johannesburg where Mandela was held in 1956 and 1962. The site is now part of the Constitution Hill precinct.

Then, in 1960, in the course of the Treason Trial, and following the Sharpeville massacre and declaration of a State of Emergency, he was again arrested and incarcerated in the Newlands prison near Sophiatown. Together with 29 others, he remained in detention – for most of the time in Pretoria Local Prison – until the lifting of the State of Emergency five months later. Before their release, the ANC was banned and would remain so for the next 30 years.
In 1962 Mandela, by then advocating armed struggle and operating underground, was apprehended in Natal and charged with incitement to strike and leaving the country without a passport. He was again jailed, awaiting trial, first at the Old Fort and later in Pretoria. On 7 November 1962 he was sentenced to a total of five years' imprisonment. After six months in the Pretoria prison he was transferred to Robben Island, where he spent only a few weeks before being returned to Pretoria. The reason for the move soon became clear. Evidence of ANC involvement in a guerrilla struggle and in acts of sabotage had been uncovered and, on 11 July 1963, some members of the High Command of uMkhonto weSizwe (MK) – the ANC's military wing – and others had been arrested at Lilliesleaf farm in Rivonia. Although Mandela was already in prison at the time, he was still the commander of MK. He was brought back from Robben Island to stand trial as the Number One Accused in what became known as the Rivonia Trial.

On 12 June 1964 Mandela and seven of his fellow trialists were sentenced to life imprisonment. At 1am the following morning, all of them – except Dennis Goldberg – were herded from their cell in Pretoria Central Prison onto a small plane and flown to Robben Island, a tiny outcrop in Table Bay, off Cape Town. They would remain there for 18 years, and in some cases even longer. Goldberg, because he was white, remained in Pretoria.

In April 1982 Mandela, together with three other Rivonia trialists – Walter Sisulu, Raymond Mhlaba and Andrew Mlangeni – were moved to Pollsmoor prison in Cape Town, where they were joined by Ahmed Kathrada in October of that year. The Pollsmoor group was further divided when Mandela was moved first into a separate cell, and subsequently in 1988 into a bungalow at Victor Verster prison in Paarl, outside Cape Town. On 11 February 1990 Nelson Mandela, the last of the Rivonia trialists to be released, walked through the gates of the Victor Verster prison as a free man, to assume his role as 'President-in-Waiting'.

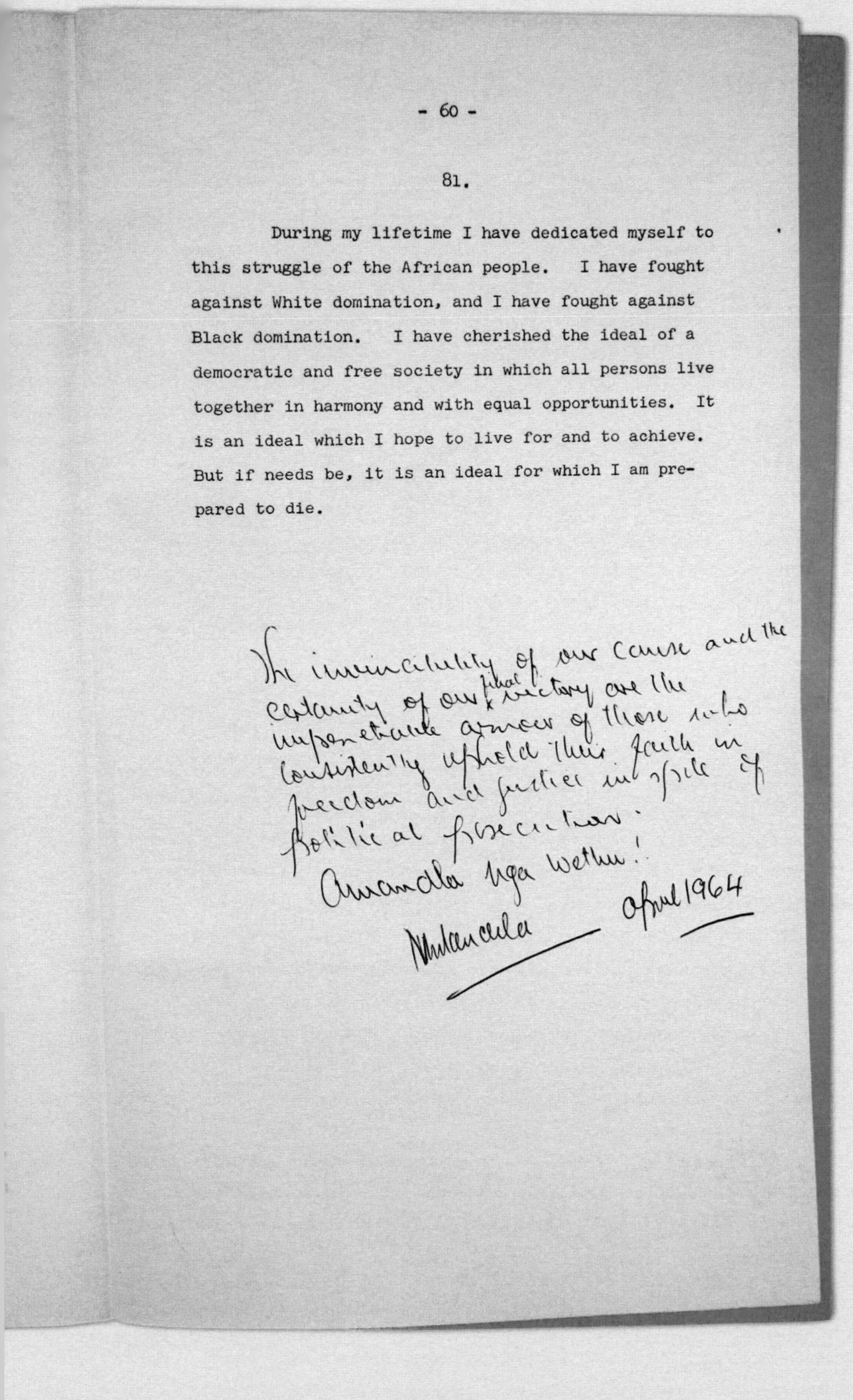

- 60 -

81.

      During my lifetime I have dedicated myself to
this struggle of the African people. I have fought
against White domination, and I have fought against
Black domination. I have cherished the ideal of a
democratic and free society in which all persons live
together in harmony and with equal opportunities. It
is an ideal which I hope to live for and to achieve.
But if needs be, it is an ideal for which I am prepared to die.

The invincibility of our cause and the certainty of our final victory are the impenetrable armour of those who consistently uphold their faith in freedom and justice inspite of political prosecution.

Amandla nga wethu!

Mandela — April 1964

Final page of Mandela's
statement from the dock
at the Rivonia Trial.

① Statement from the dock

② If I meant everything I said

③ The blood of many patriots in this country have been shed for demanding treatment in conformity with civilised standards

④ That army is being & grown

⑤ If I must die, let me declare for all to know that I will meet my fate like a man

Notes for a Death Sentence

A profound silence engulfed the courtroom when Mandela concluded his statement from the dock on 23 April 1964 with the words: 'It is an ideal which I hope to live for and to achieve. But if needs be it is an ideal for which I am prepared to die.' Seven weeks later, on 11 June 1964, the court found all the accused except Rusty Bernstein guilty, and the prospect of a death sentence loomed. The archive has yielded a brief five-point note written in a hasty scrawl by Mandela as he prepared to respond to a death sentence. In the authorised biography Anthony Sampson records that point four is difficult to read, and that even Mandela could not recall what he had written. However, on 13 August 2005 the note was again presented to Mandela by Mac Maharaj, Tim Couzens and Verne Harris. Again, a profound silence. After a long pause, Mandela read slowly '"That army ... that army ..." um "... is being and grown."' All present then agreed that it was a reference to the ANC's armed wing. And that it says either 'That army is beginning to grow' or 'That army is beginning and growing'. The reading confirms that Mandela would not have backed down in face of a death sentence. He would have stood by his 23 April statement. And he would have issued the warning that his death would not stop the liberation movement.

A question of control

During Mandela's many years of incarceration, prison authorities compiled a detailed record around prisoner 466/64. They carefully recorded, duplicated and filed every piece of paper relating to Mandela. These included results of medical tests, correspondence with family and friends, formal complaints against prison conditions and early negotiations with his captors. The prison files reveal the extent of the web of surveillance that existed in apartheid South Africa, the depth of paranoia around Mandela and, most strikingly, the power that this Robben Island prisoner wielded in spite of his status as an inmate.

Mandela's official prison record from 1964 to 1990, held at the National Archives in Pretoria, consists of 76 brown archival boxes. In each box there are one to three volumes of files, most containing well over 200 sheets of paper. By comparison, the files of fellow inmate Kathrada consist of just 26 boxes.

Mandela – official spokesperson of the group of 30 leaders held in the Isolation Section on Robben Island – was himself an avid documenter, deeply conscious of the role, and the power, of the record. As a result, his files are filled with accounts of the prisoners' engagement with the authorities over nearly three decades. In the mid-1980s, from Pollsmoor prison, Mandela began negotiations with the apartheid state, the details of which further swell the files. In addition, across the entire incarceration period the authorities monitored all media coverage relating to the prisoners, much of which focused on the figure of Mandela, and most of which is documented in some way in his files. As a result, Mandela's enormous prison record offers a unique perspective on the broad processes of repression, analysis and negotiation by the apartheid state, and on the responses and initiatives of its adversaries, over a long period. But it is far from the sum total of the Prison Archive.

Mandela's accumulated official record now housed in the National Archives, with further files located in the Cape Archives Repository, was created primarily by five different divisions of government: Prison Services, the Department of Justice, the Security Police, the State President's Office and the National Intelligence Service. Each of these state agencies established records with different objectives and concerns in mind, and sometimes even different political imperatives, and these agendas themselves shifted over the years. What was constant across the departments and over time was the effort involved in controlling that record.

The system of control began on Robben Island. A record of every one of Mandela's letters was meticulously entered into an official register by the Prison Services.

Record of Family Visits.

	Date		Name of Visitor	Duration
1	28 August 1964		Nobandla	30 minutes
2	10 July 1965		Nobandla	30 minutes
3	18 December 1965		Nobandla	30 minutes
4	6 March 1966		Late ma	30 minutes
5	9 July 1966		Nobandla	30 minutes
6	19 July 1966		Nobandla	
7	4 February '67		Mali	
8	17 June '67		Nobandla	
9	19 June '67		Joel Carlson	1 hour
10	9 September '67		Late ma	1 hour
11	7 October '67		Kgatho	1 hour
12	12 November '67		David Madau	1 hour
13	30 December '67		Sibali Manyawuza	1 hour
14	3 February 1968	Room 264 waitroom	Ntrana Mxakeki	1 hour
15	3 March 1968		Nobandla	1 hour
16	11 May 1968		Sister Mabel Timakwe	30 minutes
17	29 June 1968		Kgatho	1 hour
18	21 September 1968		Nobandla	1 hour
19	21 December 1968		Nobandla	1 hour
21	12 October 1968		Timothy Mbazo	1 hour
22	28 June 1969		Moosa Dinath fails to turn up	—
	2 June 1969		Alfred Mgulwa fails to turn up	—
20	9 August 1969		Contact visit with Mr Moosa Dinath	1 hour
21	6 September 1969		Tellie	1 hour
22	25 October 1969		Kgatho	1 hour
23	29 November 1969		Lulu	1 hour
24	27 December 1969		Thoko	1 hour
25	31 January 1970		Kgatho	1 hour
26	23 April 1970		Thoko	30 minutes

Besoeke 1988

G.P.-S. 005-0320

SA GEVANGENISDIENS
SA PRISONS SERVICE

G 367

OPGAAF VAN BRIEWE GESKRYF/BRIEWE EN BESOEKE ONTVANG
RECORD OF LETTERS WRITTEN/LETTERS AND VISITS RECEIVED

Hierdie vorm moet gebruik word vir alle gevangenes en moet die gevangene by oorplasing vergesel
This form to be used for all prisoners and to accompany the grisoner on transfer

Gevangenis Prison	Pollsmoor / /	Groep Group	Datum Date	Groep Group	Datum Date
Nommer Number	D.220/82 /				
Naam Name	Nelson Mandela		A 86/10/0		

Datum brief/besoek ontvang Date letter/ visit received	Datum brief geskryf Date letter written	Naam en adres van besoeker/afsender/geadresseerde Name and address of visitor/sender/addressee	Duur van besoek Duration of visit	Paraat van lid Initials of member	Nagesien deur Checked by
30 88.01.16	K/SEUN	MANDLA MANDELA, 8115 ORLANDO WEST	40MIN	B.	
29 88.01.17	K/SEUN	MANDLA MANDELA, 8115 ORLANDO WEST	40MIN	B	
28 88.01.24	K/DOG	N. MANDELA ; UCT; RONDEBOSH	40MIN	B	
88.01.28	PROK.	H. BERNADT, 14 LONG STR, C.T.	40MIN	B	S/BESOEK
✓ 27 88.02.01	PROK.	P. JANA, 51 COMMISIONER STR, J.H.B	40MIN	B	
26 88.2.16	VROU	N. MANDELA 8115 ORLANDO WEST	40 m.	B	
25 88.2.27	VRIENDIN K/DOG	N. MANDELA + G. MADASA U.C.T.	40 m.	B.	
24 88.3.10	PROK + VROU	I. AYOB + D AYOB JOHANNESBURG	40 m	B	
23 88.3.10	" "	" "	40 m	B	
22 88.04.04	SUSTER	L PILISO, P/BAG 13, HALFWAY HOUSE	40MIN	B	
21 88.04.25	SUSTER/KIND	N TONTO MANDELA, 856 ORLANDO, J.H.B	40MIN	B	
20 88.04.25	SUSTER/KIND	NTO-VTO MANDELA, 856 ORLANDO, J.H.B	40MIN	B	
✓ 19 88.05.02	PROK.	P. JANA, 51 COMMISIONER STR, J.H.B.	40MIN	B	
18 88.05.14	VROU/K. DOG	W & N MANDELA, 8115 ORLANDO WEST	40 MIN	B	
17 88.05.14	VROU/K DOG	W & N MANDELA, 8115 ORLANDO WEST	40MIN	B	
16 88.5.21	SUSTER	M. TIMAKWE " "	40 m.	B.	
15 88.06.12	K/DOG	N & N MANDELA, COURT 4, ROOM 111, ROND	40 MIN	B	
14 88.06.30	S/KIND	P PILISO; P/BAG X314; MOUNT FRERE	40 MIN	B	
13 88.06.30	S/KIND	P. PILISO, P/BAG X314; MOUNT FRERE	40MIN	B	
12 88.07.23	VRIEND	Y XA CACHALIA, " X312, J.H.B	40 MIN	B	
11 88.07.23	VRIEND	ROBERT BROWN U.S.A.	40MIN	B	
	VROU	WINNIE MANDELA, 8115 ORLANDO	40MIN		
	DOG	ZINDZI MANDELA, 8115 ORLANDO			
10 88.07.23	VROU/DOG	W & Z MANDELA, 8115 ORLANDO	40MIN	B	
9 88.07.24	VRIENDIN	M. RAMPHELE, 27 RALEIGH RD, MORREY	40MIN	B	
8 88.07.25	VRIENDIN	T. MATANZIMA U.C.T.	—	B.	
88.07.28	PROK	I. AYOB & PARTNERS, J.H.B	150MIN	B	R/Besoek
88.07.30	PROK	I. AYOB & PARTNERS, J.H.B	15 MIN	B	R/BESOEK
7 88.08.03	VROU/DOG	W & Z MANDELA, 8115 ORLANDO, SOWETO	40MIN	B	
6 88.08.03	VROU/DOG	W & Z MANDELA, 8115 ORLANDO, SOWETO	40MIN	B	
5 88.11.10	PROK	R TUCKER; TU DELVERS SQR, JHB	120MIN	B	R/Besoek
		BESOEKE TE VICTOR VERSTER.			
88.12.08	MIN.	Brig. U ZYL, Kol CROSSEN + MIN.		B	

Inskrywings op hierdie vorm moet deur lede van die SA Gevangenisdiens gemaak word
The entries on this form should be made by members of the SA Prisons Service

██
██
████████████ "

Your remarks about the last trial and the present are quite appropriate and highly appreciated." ███████████████████████████████

██
██
██
██
██
██
████████████████████. I wondered if such a man ever
worries about his epitaph, priding himself as he does over his grandfather's
epitaph. I remembered not without pathos rather than bitterness that
this is the absurd mind which argues that separate development
is the magna carta of the african people but what on earth does
he achieve by lying to himself? if anything it makes my task so
much easier,

I was reminded of a peasant's speech I once read, an old man
who had never seen the door of a classroom ████████████████
██████████████████████ My lord hears I shot at an aero-
plane with an arrow, he laughs, I laugh too, he thinks it's funny
and so do I — when a man tells me he is stronger than the whole
world I laugh, I think it's too funny." He was facing the same charges
I now face for having said to a state witness whilst driving past the
Orlando stadium, looking at a football crowd — that they would be better
off as soldiers instead of playing football — perhaps the most
terroristic of all my so called terroristic activities is saying to the
same poor soul — "that I would fight in the front line when the
revolution started" this recurs in the present indictment.

LEFT AND OPPOSITE:

Censored letters from

Mandela's prison file.

In some cases the original letter was returned to the prisoner with instructions to rewrite, excluding the sections crossed out by prison authorities. In some cases, the entire letter had been crossed out. Each letter was then typed up by the authorities, with censored portions indicated by rows of dots. The typewritten copies remained in Mandela's prison file, together with photocopies – once photocopiers were introduced – of the handwritten letters, all incoming letters and original letters that were never sent or were never given to Mandela.

In the 1960s, Mandela and the other prisoners were allowed to write and receive one letter, of a maximum of 500 words, every six months. Over the years, the restrictions on letter writing were relaxed and Mandela's correspondence grew. By 1975, he was allowed three letters a month. After he was moved to Pollsmoor in 1982, he could write and receive 52 letters a year. Only in exceptional circumstances were prisoners allowed to correspond with persons not in their immediate families.

PRISONS DEPARTMENT
Vermeulen House;
Vermeulen Street;

VERTROULIK
CONFIDENTIAL

PRETORIA

Private Bag 136,
Telephone: 3-7451
Telegraphic address: "Komvang"

The Commanding Officer,
Prison Command,
Private Bag,
R O B B E N   I S L A N D.
7400

Your reference	1/3/13:	21-3- 19 74
My reference	Ser.No. 913:	8-4- 19 74
Enquiries	SECURITY	Ext. 25

re

:   LETTER N. MANDELA : MRS. H. SUZMAN.

Please inform the abovenamed that his letter addressed
to Mrs. H. Suzman via Nkisikazi Nobandla Mandela of
Orlando West has not been released.

The letter has since been placed on his file for
safe keeping.

GEVANGENIS
BEVELVOERENDE OFFICIER
PRIVAATSAK/PRIVATE BAG
17 -4- 1974
ROBBENEILAND/ROBBEN ISLAND
OFFICER COMMANDING
PRISON

COMMISSIONER OF PRISONS

① Head of Prison.
   Inform prisoner Mandela
   accordingly. Informed on 18/4/74

② Censors.
   File on his letters folder
   please.

17/4/74.

This document and the two that follow tell a story of censorship and bureaucracy, relating to
attempts by Mandela to get a letter to Member of Parliament Helen Suzman in 1974.

8115 Orlando West,
P.O. Orlando.
8.5.74.

The Commanding Officer,
Department of Prisons,
ROBBEN ISLAND.

Dear Sir,

On the 13.4.74 when I saw my husband he advised me that amongst
the letters he wrote were two I have not yet received to date. The two were mine
for the month of February which he told me he had to re-write because he was
advised his writing was invisible. The other one was seeming addressed C/O myself
for Mrs. Hellen Suzman.

I have noticed the improvement in correspondence between my husband
and the family and am happy about it. I am sure he is also happy about it, this
we thank you for.

I would be grateful if you could check on the two letters with my
husband and forward them at your earliest convenience.

Yours faithfully,

Nomzamo W. Mandela.

Colonel,
The prisoners' full quota of letters were
posted during February. The letter to Dr. H. Suzman
was not approved of. (H.Q.). Mandela was informed
accordingly and at the time of the visit he was well awa
of this. [signature]
20/5/74.

Censors.
This record of letters received + written +
discuss with me please [signature]
21/5/74.

The Officer Commanding,

Prison Command,

Private Bag, ROBBEN ISLAND.
                7400

Mrs. W. Mandela,   Serial No. 913   4.6. 74
8115 Orlando West,
P.O. Orlando.
JOHANNESBURG.   11   31

NELSON MANDELA 466/64 : LETTERS

Madam,

        Your letter dated 8th instant refers.

        A special letter was granted to your husband in
lieu of the letter you did not receive during February
1974.   This letter was posted on 21st May, 1974.

        The letter he wrote to Dr. H. Suzman was not re-
leased and he was informed accordingly.

        Yours faithfully,

J. H. KRÜGER
OFFICER COMMANDING

Letters that were deemed political in nature were withheld from the prisoners. Certain of the prisoners' letters were, likewise, never forwarded. The few letters that Mandela's correspondents eventually received had already been grubbied by countless hands and processes. Portions were blackened out and, in some cases, sections of letters were physically excised. In a letter of 19 November 1979 to the Minister of Police and Prisons, Mandela complained: 'The final point I should like you to examine is the manner in which the letters I write to my wife are handled in transit. She informs me that many of them reach her in a mutilated or illegible condition. According to her, some of them appear to have been treated with chemicals …'

Many of the letters were, in fact, composed by the prisoners with the intention that they be read by people other than those to whom they were specifically addressed. This was because of the restrictions on the numbers of letters that could be written (a single letter often contained messages and instructions for a number of people), the limits set by the security establishment on the nature of permissible communication, and a recognition that the letters could be used effectively as reports on their incarceration. Though for the most part written in a private tone, as letters composed in prison they were destined for the invasive eye of the censor, political evaluation by agents of the apartheid government, decoding by informers and security policemen in search of hidden meanings and endless other unintended diversions. Likewise, forms and registers recorded every visit ever paid to the prisoners. In the early years, visits were severely restricted, with the prisoners allowed two visits a year of half an hour each. Mandela saw his wife, Winnie, for the first time in August 1964 and then not again for two years. In 1968 he saw his son Makgatho and daughter Makaziwe for the first time since the 1964 trial.

A panoply of regulations surrounded the visits. The minimum age for visitors was 16, so Mandela did not see his other daughters, Zeni and Zindzi, until December 1975 – 11 years after he had been sentenced.

In the half-hour encounters with his family, Mandela, like all political prisoners, was forbidden to touch them, to speak to them in his home language of Xhosa or to discuss people outside the immediate family. Husband and wife shouted to each other through the glass partition with warders listening in and watching on both sides.

A visitors' room on
Robben Island. Initially
political prisoners were
only allowed two visits a
year of half an hour each.

ABOVE: **A photograph of Winnie that Mandela kept in his Robben Island cell.**

OPPOSITE: **Winnie and Zeni Mandela before Mandela's imprisonment.**

By 1975 Mandela was allowed two visits a month by 'first-degree family members', but they would involve no physical contact at all, even though he was officially entitled to this. He received regular contact visits only from 1986 when he was in Pollsmoor and had been moved to a separate section, away from his comrades. From 1986 all these prisoners were allowed contact visits, including visits by children. By the time he was in Victor Verster, Mandela was instructing the prison authorities as to whom he wanted to consult and for how long. They acceded to his requests as part of the process of negotiations.

Despite its volume, and the intensity of the state's concern to establish the record, the official files now concentrated in the National Archives are, in the main, haphazardly arranged and poorly catalogued. Some files are simply chaotic. Individual documents can be difficult to locate. Many pages are disintegrating and those in photocopy or fax form are fading. The Centre of Memory is negotiating to initiate a joint project with the National Archives to arrange and conserve the papers.

Ironically, the doggedness of the regime in recording Mandela's every word and every move ensured an extraordinarily rich record of his years in captivity. This record affords us a unique insight into the psychological, social and political world of his incarceration – his relationships with the warders, with his fellow prisoners, with his own internal world as well as with the world outside. It is not just a record of his imprisonment, but also that of the birth of democracy in South Africa. It is that Prison Archive, combined with Mandela's experiences of life before prison, that enabled the passionate freedom fighter who entered jail in 1962 to emerge with the capacity to lead a remarkable process of reconciliation and justice.

OPPOSITE:

Zeni and Zindzi at about the time they were first permitted to visit their father on Robben Island.

THE BULLETIN

Inco... The Austra...

WORL EXCLUSIV

Insi
Sout
Africa
worst ja

David McNicoll talks to the key political prisoners.

Beyond Mandela's prison files

The wider Prison Archive for the 1964–1990 period is spread across the official records of his fellow inmates, their memories, stories and private archives, the elements of their correspondence in the hands of those to whom they wrote, the material traces of their incarcerations − including their cells and the objects that so many of them have donated for display in those cells − and the records of the numerous lawyers who had dealings with the prisoners. There are also the memories of the people who visited the prisoners − family, lawyers, doctors and, in Mandela's case, friends and comrades − and the people who guarded them. The wider Prison Archive confirms some elements of Mandela's Prison Archive and, in other respects, offers entirely different perspectives. The total Prison Archive is an immensely rich and diverse body of material.

Media documentation and stories are one element of the wider Prison Archive, outside the official files, although often also documented in the official files. In 1964, a few weeks after the Rivonia trialists arrived on Robben Island, a journalist from the UK's *Daily Telegraph* was allowed to photograph the prisoners and captured Mandela in conversation with Walter Sisulu.

The prisoners, however, were well aware that the South African government countered international coverage with carefully orchestrated media visits to Robben Island, and became increasingly angered by the propaganda. In 1973 the government invited David McNicoll of an Australian weekly, *The Bulletin*, to South Africa, where he visited the Island and spoke to the prisoners. There were no contemporary photographs accompanying his account.

But the media archive was not controlled entirely by the state, and this is especially true of the international media. Official documents relating to Mandela's 60th birthday, celebrated on 18 July 1978, are sparse. He received only eight messages from family and friends, although anti-apartheid campaigners spearheaded from Britain sent him 10 000 birthday cards that never arrived. The international press covered the occasion extensively.

While published or broadcast materials are relatively easy to locate, unpublished or unedited materials are more elusive. In 2004, on condition of anonymity, a researcher approached the Centre of Memory with a collection of over 30 photographs taken on Robben Island in 1977, including the various 'prisoner in the garden' images. The Centre established that most of the photographs had been taken during the course of a visit to Robben Island by a group of journalists, organised by the apartheid government seeking to dispel rumours of harsh conditions on the Island. The Centre determined that the photographs are a copy of an official set transferred to the National Archives by the Department of Correctional Services.

OPPOSITE:

Front cover of Australian magazine *The Bulletin*, April 1973.

A number of the photographs bore the distinctive mark of censorship, notably blacked-out faces of the prisoners. Articles about the visit appeared in newspapers only two days later to allow time for all texts and images to be approved by the state.

They stand in groups, neatly togged in prison garb, both inside and outside the confines of the prison wall and fences. They wear dark glasses, many of them, and hats. They grow beards, if doctors prescribe it.

The tempo of their work – weeding, raking and scoffling [sic] in the sandy soil – is slow, like the island as a whole. Slow.

This was the group including Nelson Mandela, leader of the banned African National Congress, sentenced to life imprisonment in 1964 for sabotage and plotting to overthrow the state by revolution.

Mandela, now aged 59, wearing dark glasses and a floppy hat, was not pleased with a visit to the prison by the Press.
(*The Star*, 27 April 1977)

While the photographs of Mandela's cell and other scenes from Robben Island were published in local newspapers (always with the faces of prisoners blacked out), the images of Mandela himself were suppressed in terms of contemporary prison legislation. Most of the photographs reproduced here have never before been seen in public.

The discovery of this set of images led to the recovery of film footage of the 1977 visit held by the South African Broadcasting Corporation (SABC). The footage, it seems, had never been flighted, or at least not in this form, and had remained uncatalogued, gathering dust in the SABC's archives. In fact, it only surfaced following a chance recollection of the archivist who remembered noticing canisters marked 'Robben Island'.

The images from the 1977 visit reveal that, on the eve of his 60th birthday and in the middle of his jail term, the prison experience was shaping Mandela into a man with a manifestly strong spirit who embodied authority.

OPPOSITE:

Journalists take notes during a visit to Robben Island in 1977.

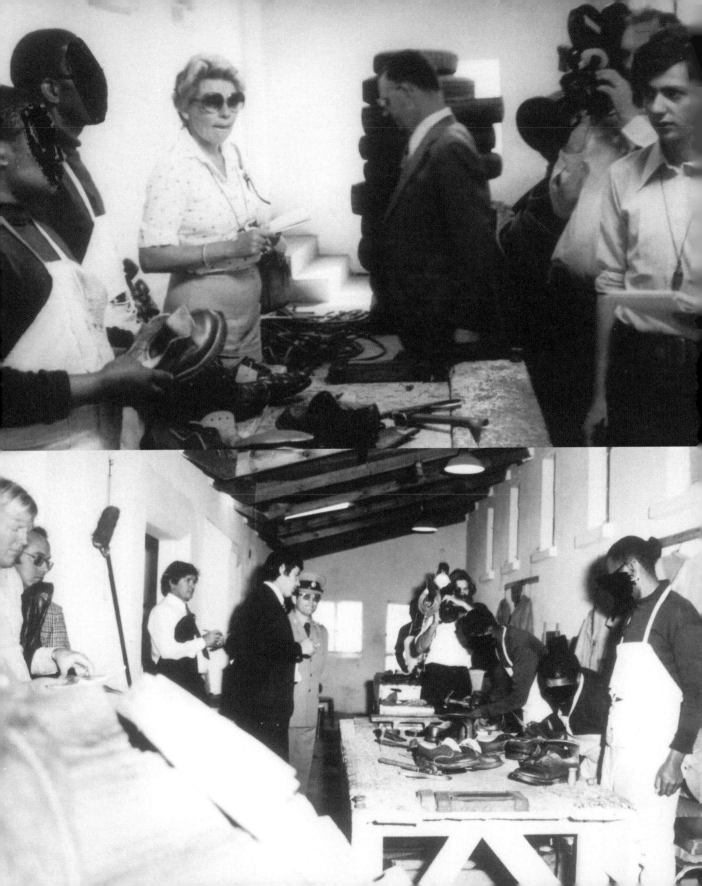

Photographs from 1977
media visit to Robben
Island. The faces of
inmates were blacked out
by the prison authorities
before the photographs
were released for
publication.

NO. 466/64 NELSON

NDELA D 220/82

1335/88: Nelson M

gene nommer 913

Many Prison Numbers

The prison number most commonly associated with Mandela is 466/64, recently popularised by the Nelson Mandela Foundation's 46664 HIV/AIDS campaign. In fact, as one would expect from a petty and pedantic bureaucracy, Mandela had many prison numbers. The number 466/64 was his Robben Island number, as the 466th person to be incarcerated here in 1964. His Pollsmoor number was 220/82, and his Victor Verster number 1335/88. Throughout the period from 1964 to 1990, he carried the prison file number 913. Closer examination, no doubt, would reveal others ...

Mandela's long-time
comrades Mac Maharaj
(left) and Ahmed Kathrada
at the exhibition launch in
September 2004.
PREVIOUS:
Donald Card handing
over the notebooks
to Mandela.

FAMILY
CORRESPONDE
- NCE

CHAPTER THREE

An Unlocking of Story
The archival threads connecting two old men

At the opening of the *466/64: A Prisoner Working in the Garden* exhibition on 21 September 2004, two notebooks taken from Nelson Mandela while he was in prison were personally returned to him by the former security policeman in whose hands they ended up. Short speeches were given by Mandela; the former policeman Donald Card; Chief Executive of the Nelson Mandela Foundation John Samuel; and Ahmed Kathrada, Mandela's close comrade and former fellow prisoner. Over 150 guests and a large media contingent were in attendance. The event was webcast live around the world, and staff of the Nelson Mandela Centre of Memory and Commemoration and a historian were available to answer questions. Kathrada recalled the words of Colonel Aucamp of Prison Services, spoken at the beginning of the prisoners' long incarceration. Aucamp promised the prisoners that their isolation on Robben Island would be so complete that within five years no one would remember who they were. The inauguration of the Centre 40 years later was eloquent testimony to the power of memory in the face of coercive force.

Mandela drew attention to the significance of the return of the two notebooks, linking them to the 'call of justice' that lies at the heart of the Centre of Memory.

Good afternoon everybody. I thank you for attending this function at the invitation of an old man. What you have just witnessed could be described as one old man giving another old man two old notebooks. And let me at once thank Mr Card for returning these items to me. However, I want you to see the symbolic significance of this event. Under the apartheid regime it was a common practice for the authorities to take documents from those they regarded as enemies. Sometimes they used these documents as evidence in court cases. Sometimes they used them in various forms of intimidation. Sometimes they simply destroyed them. For all of us who were part of the struggles for justice and freedom in this country, committing information to paper was a very risky business. We had to be careful about how we did this, and careful about what we kept and where we kept it. (I obviously wasn't careful enough with the notebooks!)

This reality in itself was a form of intimidation. And one of the results is that today there are relatively few archives documenting the thinking and the inner processes of the liberation movements.

OPPOSITE:

A page from Mandela's notebooks recovered in 2004.

So we invite you to see these notebooks as more than just the working documents of a prisoner. They represent the hope that we can recover memories and stories suppressed by the apartheid regime. Mr Card might easily have decided to destroy the notebooks, or sell them to a wealthy collector in this country or from some other country. We remind you that there are many people who once worked in apartheid structures who today have documents in their cupboards or their garages or in a safe place overseas. That is part of our unfinished business of dealing with the past and ensuring that restoration takes place. Mr Card is to be commended for his contribution to restoration and reconciliation.

In our view the work of archives in the South Africa of today is potentially one of the critical contributions to restoration and reconciliation. All of us have a powerful moral obligation to the many voices and stories either marginalised or suppressed during the apartheid era.

Today we are launching the Nelson Mandela Centre of Memory Project. We want it to be part of what we have called the processes of restoration and reconciliation. The two notebooks given to me today by Mr Card will be the first acquisitions for this Centre of Memory. It is our hope that from these small beginnings it will grow into a vibrant public resource offering a range of services to South Africans and visitors from all parts of the world. We want it to work closely with the many other institutions which make up the South African archival system. And, most importantly, we want it to dedicate itself to the recovery of memories and stories suppressed by power. That is the call of justice. The call which must be the project's most important shaping influence.

The history of our country is characterised by too much forgetting. A forgetting which served the powerful and dispossessed the weak. (Of course there are other forms of forgetting. As a very old man now I have been forced to make friends with forgetting.) One of our challenges as we build and extend democracy is the need to ensure that our youth know where we come from, what we have done to break the shackles of oppression, and how we have pursued the journey to freedom and dignity for all. We will fail our youth if we leave them in ignorance of what has given them the opportunities which they enjoy. At the same time, for those of us who are older and have lived through the transition from apartheid to democracy, the processes of remembering offer us healing and a means of respecting the many comrades who made it possible.

This is what archive is about. This is what we want the Centre of Memory Project to be about. We will be grateful for any assistance in helping us to achieve this objective. I thank you.

(Nelson Mandela, 21 September 2004)

Detail of Mandela's
Robben Island cell.

'One old man giving another old man two old notebooks...' With these words, the world's most famous ex-prisoner, Nelson Mandela, received from Donald Card, former security policeman, two black-jacketed notebooks written by Mandela during his incarceration on Robben Island. In accepting the books originally seized from him, Mandela repeated the act of reconciliation that marked South Africa's transition to democracy. In restoring the books to their author, the other old man set right a past wrong. And in the safe custody of the Centre of Memory, the two old notebooks assumed the status of archival documents.

That is how the media reported the event. They focused on the reunion of notebooks and owner, on Card's decision to preserve the notebooks and efforts to return them, and on the notebooks as the first acquisitions of the Centre. The events of the day offered some clue – provided by the ex-prisoners, the former security policeman, the historian and the staff of the Centre of Memory – to the deeper stories linked to the handover. Had the media attempted to tease out the archival threads entangled around the event they might have drawn the public's attention to the meaning of 'archives for social justice'. As in every archival tale, the truth as reported in the media was itself provisional, subject to expansion, revision and reinterpretation. One document always leads to another; one truth always opens a realm of further possibilities. The enigmas, silences and contradictions in the record are often signs of further stories to be investigated. And the safety of the repository is not guaranteed by the weight of the key!

The notebooks

Examination of the two old notebooks reveals archival threads spreading in many directions. The notebooks contain original drafts of 79 letters composed by Nelson Mandela in the period April 1969 to April 1971. The notebooks were, of course, not available to Mandela when he wrote his autobiography published in 1994. Indeed, he did not remember the notebooks when they were first shown to him. Careful review leaves no doubt as to their authenticity, and many of the letters in the notebooks are referred to nowhere else in the record around Mandela. Once Mandela had rewritten the drafts on notepaper, these were then submitted to the prison authorities for censorship and mailing onwards. The letters were copied by the authorities for the prison record, and on occasion duplicated for the records of other government departments. Outgoing letters, like the similarly censored incoming correspondence, were then meticulously recorded in lists that were carefully filed. Letters written in this period were forwarded to Donald Card for decoding, after which he mailed them onwards. That, at least, was how the system was supposed to work. What actually happened – what acts of omission and commission occurred, how the system changed over time, and the vagaries of the involvement of particular individuals – awaits thorough investigation. There are anomalies everywhere: did Card decode already-censored letters? If he did, then perhaps he missed pieces of intelligence obscured by the black pen of the censor. If he received uncensored letters, then did those letters escape the surveillance system completely when he mailed them on? One thing is clear: the period covered by the notebooks was a time in which much original correspondence went astray. But the letters written and received were nevertheless critically important for both Mandela and many of his correspondents:

To continue writing holds out the possibility that one day luck may be on our side in that you may receive these letters. In the meantime the mere fact of writing down my thoughts and expressing my feelings gives me a measure of pleasure and satisfaction. It is some means of passing on to you my warmest love and good wishes, and tends to calm down the shooting pains that hit me whenever I think of you... The dream of every family is to live together happily in a quiet peaceful home where parents will have the opportunity of bringing up their children in the best possible way, of guiding and helping them in choosing careers and of giving them love and care which will develop in them a feeling of serenity and self-confidence. Today our family has been scattered: Mummy and Daddy are in jail and you live like orphans. We should like you to know that these ups and downs have deepened our love for you. We are confident that one day our dreams will come true; we will be able to live together and enjoy all the sweet things that we are missing at present.

Tons and tons of love, my darlings, Daddy.
(Nelson Mandela to his daughters Zeni and Zindzi, 1 June 1970)

My Darlings,   1st June 1970.

It is now more than 8 years since I last saw you, and just over 12 months since mummy was suddenly taken away from you.

Last year I wrote you 2 letters — one on the 23rd June and the other on the 3rd August. I now know that you never received them. As both of you are still under 18, and as you are not allowed to visit me until you reach that age, writing letters is the only means I have of keeping in touch with you and of hearing something about the state of your health, your schoolwork and your school progress generally. Although these precious letters do not reach, I shall keep on trying nevertheless by writing whenever that is possible. I am particularly worried by the fact that for more than a year I received no clear and first-hand information as to who looks after you during school holidays and where you spend such holidays, who feeds you and buys you clothing, who pays your school fees, board and lodging, and on the progress that you are making at school. To continue writing holds out the possibility that one day luck may be on our side in that you may receive these letters. In the meantime the mere fact of writing down my thoughts and expressing my feelings gives me a measure of pleasure and satisfaction. It is some means of passing on to you my warmest love and good wishes, and tends to calm down the shooting pains that hit me whenever I think of you.

In the first letter I told you that mummy was a brave woman who is suffering today because she deeply loves her people and her country. She had chosen the life of misery and sorrow in order that you, Zeni and Zindzi, Maki and Kgatho, and many others like you might grow up and live peacefully and happily in a free country where all the people, black and white, would be bound together by a common loyalty to a new South Africa. I gave you a brief account of her family background and career and the many occasions in which she has been sent to jail. I ended the letter by giving you the assurance that one day mummy and I would return and join you perhaps at 8115 Orlando West or may be in some other "home." It may well be that she may come back with her poor health worse than it is at present and needing much nursing and care. It will then be your turn to look after her. Your love and affectionate devotion will serve to heal the deep and ugly wounds caused by many years of hardship and may prolong her life indefinitely. The second letter contained the sad news of the death of Buti Thembi in a car accident near Cape Town and I gave you deepest sympathy on behalf of mummy and me. I do hope that some good friend was able to

[left margin, vertical text, partially legible:]
"Make sure we again last Saturday. She had been battling for a permit since the first week of February. I suggest that you immediately apply by register a letter for a permit, and indicate the exact date when you would like to visit me, pointing out at the same time that you are a student and can only afford to come down during holidays."

The period covered by the notebooks was one of concentrated anguish for Mandela, encompassing as it did the death of his mother and then his eldest son Thembekile.

I find it difficult to believe that I will never see Thembi again. On February 23 this year, he turned 24. I had seen him towards the end of July 1962, a few days after I had returned from the trip abroad. Then he was a lusty lad of 17 that I could never associate with death. He wore one of my trousers which was a shade too big and long for him. The incident was significant and set me thinking. As you know he had a lot of clothing, was particular about his dress and had no reason whatsoever for using my clothes. I was deeply touched for the emotional factors underlying his action were too obvious.

(Nelson Mandela to Zami [Winnie], 16 July 1969)

In the same period, Winnie Mandela was detained. Beyond his anxiety about the fate of his wife, the situation of the children was desperately distressing. Not only were the young children deprived of parental care, but the imprisoned parents were unable to communicate with the children and possible guardians, and struggled to make arrangements for their wellbeing, and for the management of other domestic affairs.

Then came '68 and '69 when the skies suddenly fell upon me. I lost both him [Thembi] and Ma and I must confess that the order that had reigned in my soul almost vanished. Exactly two months before Thembi's death my Zami was put under lock and key where she still is, and our household affairs plunged into unbelievable chaos. Up to the present moment I do not know where Zeni and Zindzi (aged 11 and 10 respectively) are and who maintains them. Every one of the letters I have written them in the last 15 months has not reached. Probably the car and furniture have been repossessed and the telephone disconnected. My funds have been completely drained...

(Nelson Mandela to Mofumahadi Zukiswa Matji, 1 August 1970)

All that notwithstanding, Mandela concluded 'My fist is firm'.

Few of the letters ever reached their destinations. In the letters contained in the two notebooks, Mandela meticulously tracked receipt of his letters and documented which of the letters he had written were never received. His anguish around the failure of the formal prison correspondence system – to which he adhered in every respect – is palpable throughout the notebooks' correspondence.

OPPOSITE:

Mandela and his eldest son Thembekile, who died in 1969 at age 24.

We are extremely disturbed because, since Zami's detention in May last year, we have heard nothing about them ... I have written them three letters and sent a birthday card, but none seems to have reached. Please investigate and give me a detailed report, preferably by registered letter, at your earliest possible convenience.

Letters from me hardly ever reach destination and those addressed to me fare no better. I am hoping that the remorseless fates, that consistently interfered with my correspondence and that have cut me off from my family at such a critical moment, will be induced by consideration of honour and honesty to allow this one through.

(Nelson Mandela to Senator Douglas Lukhele, in Swaziland, 1 August 1970)

ABOVE:
Mandela's mother,
Nosekeni Fanny, with a
photograph of her son.
OPPOSITE:
Letter to Mofumahadi
Zukiswa Matji.

Our dear Zuki,   August 1, 1970.

The death of Thembi was a bitter blow to me for he was an intimate friend. The relationship of father & son was but the foundation stone upon which we were building more intimate connections & it really hurt me to know that I would never see him again

There was a time during the last 8 years when nothing could ever ruffle me or when I felt serene & in perfect control of myself. Thembi was gradually taking over the family responsibilities & was helpful in many ways. He had become very attached to zami & kgatho & to the 2 sisters he had become an idol. Then came '68 & '69 when the skies suddenly fell upon me. I lost both him & mac & I must confess that the order that had reigned in my soul almost vanished. Exactly 2 months before Thembi's death my zami was put under lock & key where she still is, & our household affairs plunged into unbelievable chaos. Up to the present moment I do not know where zeni & zindzi [aged 11 & 10 respectively] are, who maintains them. Every one of the letters I have written them in the last months has not reached. Probably the cos have been repossessed & the telephone disconnected. My funds have been completely drained & I have had to give up a couple of necessaries which make life here comparatively easy. I cannot even manage an eye test for reading glasses. At times I am tempted to feel that this is too heavy a cross to carry. It is against this background that I regard Robbie's cheerful letter. Its warmth & simplicity touched my heart & raised my spirits.

Robbie refers to Thembi & Kgatho's visit when you were at Sekake's. What a strange coincidence. The letter arrived when I was reading about old times in Lesotho, Matatiele, Qacha's Nek & Kokstad; about Sekake, his father Sekwati & Lehana, Ou hetsie, Lerotholi & Masupha, Mhlontlo & Mditshwa, Makawula, Sofo & Mgikela. In the past 8 years I have read more on S.a. history & geography than I ever did in my whole life & this has made me curious & anxious to tour the country & to visit all the places which have aroused my interest. I do not know how I will ever raise the funds for that purpose. I have always been more needy than the proverbial church mouse, & the position will certainly be much worse on my return. However, remote problems can have no bearing on my present hobby of castle building. But this strange coincidence Zuki! Sekake & Sekake's. Is it possible that research, experiment & observation may establish telepathy as an empirical study?

The death of Masango & Moroyi was a terrible tragedy which sorely affected us. Robbie must have found it extremely painful not to be able to pay his last respects to such dedica ted fighters. Jimmy & Louie are wonderful people for whom I have the highest regard. Some of the most pleasant moments in my life were spent in their company. In the early fifties Jimmy was hot & sharp & attracted great interest. Later he seemed to cool off & the knife-edge sharpness that once I have noticed

In June I learnt for the first time that you had been confined to bed for two months ...
Is your silence due to your worsening health or did the July letter suffer the fate of the 39
monthly letters, letters in lieu of visits and specials that I have written since your arrest
on May 12, '69, all of which, save two, seemed not to have reached their destination ...
I am becoming increasingly uneasy every day.

(Nelson Mandela to Winnie, 1 August 1970)

On June 19 Brig. Aucamp explained that another department had instructed him not to
forward these letters, adding at the same time that he was not in a position to give me
reasons for these instructions, but that such instructions were not influenced by the
content of the letters. This revelation solved the riddle of the mysterious disappearance
of most of the letters I wrote over the past 15 months. The matter entails even more
serious implications. I should like to be in the position where I could always rely on
what officials tell me, but I'm finding it increasingly difficult to square up wishes with
experience. Twice during July and early this month, I was informed that your letter had
not arrived. I have now established that the letter was actually here when I was being
given assurances to the contrary. I was also disgusted to hear from you that Marsh had
been applying for a permit to see me and that he had been informed by the prisons
department that there were long queues of visitors for me. Nothing could be further
from the truth. I had only three visits in the last eight months.

(Nelson Mandela to Winnie, 31 August 1970)

Like so much of the record around Mandela, even the most personal elements speak to much
more than his singular history. Mandela, in turn, generated his own documentary profusion,
always developing a clear record, meticulously set down on paper. Unlike the countless copies
painstakingly typed up by clerks using typewriters and carbon paper — and introducing their
own unique errors of transcription and comprehension — the letters in the notebooks, penned in
Mandela's neat, assertive script, bearing evidence of his editing processes, are poignant
testimony to the prisoner's process of composition, and are of interest also to the historian
hunting for any possible evidence of a change between first draft and final product. Yet, beyond
their capacity to offer such intimate insights, the prison notebooks might also be expected to
contain what is available elsewhere in the state files. Remarkably, the official record — all those
copies of letters, suppressed originals, and much more besides — evades consultation in many
different ways: many letters had been secreted, destroyed, lost, disordered, dilapidated, or
appropriated. It may be that some of the drafts in the two notebooks are the only copies of
letters that survive. The very presence of the notebooks demands a comparison with the official
record, drawing attention to astounding absences and elisions in the official record, and to the
many violations of the archive constantly perpetrated wherever secrecy reigns.

Dade Wethu,

August 31, 1970.

Your note of July 2 was shown to me on Aug 14 - 1 month 12 days after you wrote it. It was the sweetest of all your letters, surpassing even the very first one of Dec. 20, '62. If there was ever a letter which I desperately wished to keep, read quietly over and over again in the privacy of my cell, it was that one. But I was told to read it on the spot & was grabbed away as soon as I had reached the last line.

Brig. Aucamp attempted to justify this arbitrary procedure with the flimsy excuse that in the letter you gave his name for your address instead of your prison. He went on to explain that my letters to you were handled in exactly the same way that you were not allowed to keep them. When I pressed him for an explanation he was evasive. I realised there were important issues at stake which necessitated the making of serious inroads on your right as an awaiting-trial prisoner to write & receive letters & a curtailment of my correspondence privilege. Our letters are subject to a special censorship. The real truth is that the authorities do not want you to share the contents of the letters I write you with your colleagues there, & vice versa. To prevent this they resort to all means, fair or foul. It is possible that communications between us may be whittled down still further, at least for the duration of the trial. As you know the privilege as far as my normal monthly letters to/from friends & relations practically disappeared with your arrest. I have been trying to communicate with Ma Nobandla since January last & with Telia & Tshepo since November. On June 19 Brig. Aucamp explained that another department had instructed him not to forward these letters, adding at the same time that he was not in a position to give me the reasons for the instructions, but that such instructions were not influenced by the contents of the letters. This revelation solved the riddle of the mysterious disappearance of most of the letters I wrote over the past 13 months. The matter entails even more serious implications. I should like to be in the position where I could always rely on what officials tell me, but I'm finding it increasingly difficult to square up wishes with experience. Twice during July & early this month, I was informed that your letter had not arrived. I have now established that the letter was actually true when I was being given assurances to the contrary. I was also disgusted to hear from you that Marsh had been applying for a permit to see me & that he had been informed by the prison department that there were long queues of visitors for me. Nothing could be further from the truth. I had only 5 visits during the past 8 months - in January, April & June. It is easy to understand why they are reluctant to allow Marsh to come down. He is in touch with you & a visit from him will not suit them. By & by & the Bushie wish to cut me off from you. I have had numerous experiences of this nature & each one leaves me sad & disappointed. Incidentally I was told that you & your colleagues now enjoy better privileges. I asked for more details & was shocked to learn that even after you had been formally charged you were not allowed a change of clothing & food from outside. How can any benevolent intelligent person justify this barbarism? To the best of my knowledge & belief, as an awaiting-trial prisoner you are entitled to clean garments & to food from relations & friends. These are not privileges but legal rights. The tragedy of the whole situation is the blissful ignorance on the part of
censors asked me to shorten the letter on the ground that it exceeded 500 words

* It was compensation for the forearms things you are not deprived of - the
* It was reading anniversary & birthday cards - the little things about which you never failed to think.

British, and being his own ... story. He ... inferior to ... Chief of the ... the Contempt of Chief ... eulogy for ... nguishing ... missionaries ... writes: ... Published a ... He determina- ... these qualities ... eople and to their ... and him during ... ndrawak, ... of time and ... It is exe- ... considered ... highest Courts." ... of his Cha- ... ed to his family ... ments in a ... last and Resent ... which reveals ... fused with ... constitute ... ck man is ... hand him; ... nce. Perhaps ... others - ... the sixties ... were also year

Letter to Winnie,
31 August 1970.

The other old man...

The other old man at the handover event was Donald Card. As he was clearly not well known to the reporters, Card provided a curriculum vitae to serve as the basis for his introduction by the master of ceremonies: '1947: Joined the South African Police; 1964: Became a member of the Security Police; 1970: Became very frustrated and resigned from the Police.' His speech at the handover event, designed to account for his retention of the notebooks, placed an additional autobiographical statement on record:

I am sure everyone itches to know how these books came to be in my possession. Well, I was a detective in the Security Police at the time, when in about 1969 a young man who had served time on Robben Island came to see me and said that he could be of assistance to the police because he could read the coded messages being sent in letters from Robben Island.

[As I believed that I was fighting terrorism at the time], I immediately visited the head of the Security Police in Pretoria. He called in the head of the prison department and it was decided that the warders on Robben Island would in future send me all letters written by prisoners. Envelopes fat with letters started arriving. There was one condition: once the informer and I had scrutinised the letters, and, if necessary, had made copies, they were to be immediately resealed and reposted. With the help of the informer, I worked on the 'decoding' of the Robben Island letters for over a year.

I however became frustrated with the South African Police and at the end of 1970, I resigned. Shortly thereafter, another large envelope arrived for me from Robben Island. It contained letters and two black books. Clearly the warders had not been told of my resignation. I did not check these letters; I simply posted them. The only option open to me regarding the books was to return them from where they had come but I decided against this because I thought these were very valuable documents that could be lost or destroyed. I also realised that they were safe with me because nobody would know that I had actually kept them.

(Donald Card, 21 September 2004)

While Card's statement is intriguing, the accompanying CV barely satisfies curiosity. At the handover event, Kathrada offered a clue when he noted that Card had given evidence in the Rivonia Trial 40 years earlier. The statement and the clue, like all enigmas, invite investigation of further documents out of the archive.

OPPOSITE:

Former security policeman Donald Card with the notebooks he returned to Mandela in 2004.

In 1963 Nelson Mandela and nine others were charged with sabotage and conspiring to overthrow the apartheid government. For the many years of Mandela's incarceration, his speech from the dock – carried in full in a number of contemporary publications – was the primary record of his voice and chief source for establishing the values for which he stood. And yet the record of the trial is an elusive document with a story of its own.

The transcript of the court proceedings of 26 January 1964 confirms that the 2004 handover ceremony was not the first encounter between the two men. On that day, Donald Card appeared as a state witness. The prosecutor, Percy Yutar, led him in establishing his profile rather more fully than occurred four decades later: 'A Detective Sergeant in the South African Police, stationed at East London … for the last 16 $1/2$ years … serving with the Criminal Staff but deal[ing] with numerous political matters including riots at East London, riots in Pondoland and other ANC matters.' Card gave evidence on ANC activities in the East London region, naming countless ANC members and the operational cells of which they were members, as well as providing details of numerous acts of sabotage directed against pro-government supporters. So copious was his knowledge that he earned the nickname 'Card-index'. How did you come to know all this, the defence pressed him repeatedly. 'They admitted it all to me,' was Card's response, reiterated again and again:

[After] arrest he admitted to me … I received information … he admitted to me after arrest … I kept observation … I've got sworn statements from them … unknown to me before … only admitted to me after arrest … denied that he was a member at the time he was arrested … and only after arrest did he admit that he was a member throughout … I had him in my office on a number of occasions and he promised to give me certain information … he was the man who came to me and said that he actually attended a meeting in the bush of the ANC and that he wanted me to go with … I knew what he was up to … I knew he pretended to be an informer … they were going to try and get me to go to the bushes so that I could be shot … 51 of the 52 told me they were members of the ANC.
(Rivonia Trial transcript, pages 8-11, Donald Card's cross-examination)

Card's testimony at the Rivonia Trial conjured up a complex world of informants, sell-outs, exchanges of confidence, surveillance, confessions and plots. One such plot, according to Card, was directed against his own life. Card's evidence was an important part of the lengthy case against the Rivonia accused. A much younger Card was, at least in part, instrumental in sending a much younger Mandela to jail for 27 years.

Donald Card's house in East London where Mandela's notebooks were held.

This connection was the crux of the symbolic significance of the handover, and its implications begin to reveal the meaning and the complexity of the Centre of Memory's engagement with the notion of a call of justice.

The two old notebooks facilitate a glimpse into Card's career after his appearance at the Rivonia Trial, when he worked for the Security Police. The glimpse is not in the notebooks themselves, but in their biography. It was a story tightly controlled by Card through the tale of how he came by the notebooks, an account placed on record at the handover event and containing only minimal reference to his work with the Security Police. Beyond that, Card did not expand on his years with the security forces, simply moving on to note that after resigning from the police, he became a city councillor in East London and, during the 24 years he spent there, served three terms as mayor.

In 1989 Card was invited, along with ten other members of city councils, by the Five Freedoms Forum to join a delegation of 115 white South Africans of diverse backgrounds to journey to Lusaka in Zambia to meet with the ANC in exile. It was surely remarkable for Card to journey to the headquarters of the organisation he had so relentlessly pursued and which, he believed, had sanctioned a plan to kill him. In a highly charged moment at the Lusaka meeting, perpetrator encountered victim when Card met Steve Tshwete, whose ANC involvement he had recounted with such precision in the Rivonia Trial evidence. A delegate recalled Tshwete lifting his shirt to display the physical traces of abuse. The two men embraced and both wept.

On that day in Lusaka, one wonders whether Card recalled how in 1963 he had gained knowledge of the very particular whereabouts of Tshwete's hidden maps of what the state implied were potential ANC targets:

Yes, I took possession of those maps … I found them in the room of one Stephen Tshwete… They were hidden behind the wooden partitioning and the outside [of] the corrugated iron of his room … actually the planks had been nailed down. I had to remove those planks to find those articles nailed down under the planks.

(Rivonia Trial transcript, page 12, Donald Card's cross-examination)

At the Lusaka conference, Card attended the local government subcommission and would have been heartened by the meeting's acknowledgement that more attention needed to be paid to the potential role of white city councillors in facilitating the transition to democracy. Indeed, in 1994 Card became deputy mayor under the new East London Transitional Local Council. In 1995, his contribution was commemorated when he was granted the Freedom of the City of East London.

Following the Lusaka meeting Card, extraordinarily, was subject to yet another potential death sentence. On 10 May 1990, the East London newspaper the *Daily Dispatch* reported that his name appeared on the elimination lists of the Civil Cooperation Bureau (CCB), a South African police hit squad. Insight into CCB thinking on Card is denied to posterity as the records of this state body were systematically destroyed along with hosts of other security establishment records before the transfer of power from the apartheid state in 1994.

The record of the Truth and Reconciliation Commission (TRC) provides further detail about Card. In 1995 the commission began the work of breaking the silence around the violations of human rights that had occurred in the previous decades, allowing both victims and perpetrators an opportunity to speak. It conducted hearings across the country. In an affidavit made to the TRC, outspoken apartheid critic Donald Woods recorded how in 1977, when he was editor of the *Daily Dispatch*, a small T-shirt impregnated with a poison was posted to his five-year-old daughter. Card, whom Woods described as a family friend and a former security police officer who had turned against his former colleagues, investigated and identified the culprits as three policemen.

As a result of the investigation Card, in turn, was threatened with 'elimination' by a senior police officer, and was harassed. But this did not stop Card, along with activist lawyer and ex-Robben Islander Louis Mtshizana, and a local Catholic priest, Ted Molyneaux, from subsequently helping Woods and his family to leave the country clandestinely.

Rather surprisingly, Card requested amnesty from the TRC for this act which, while illegal at the time, by no stretch of the imagination constituted a gross violation of human rights. The request did ensure that the act was entered into the record of the TRC. Card, it seems, understood very well the relationship between power and archive. However, it was not to be the only entry in the TRC archive concerning Card.

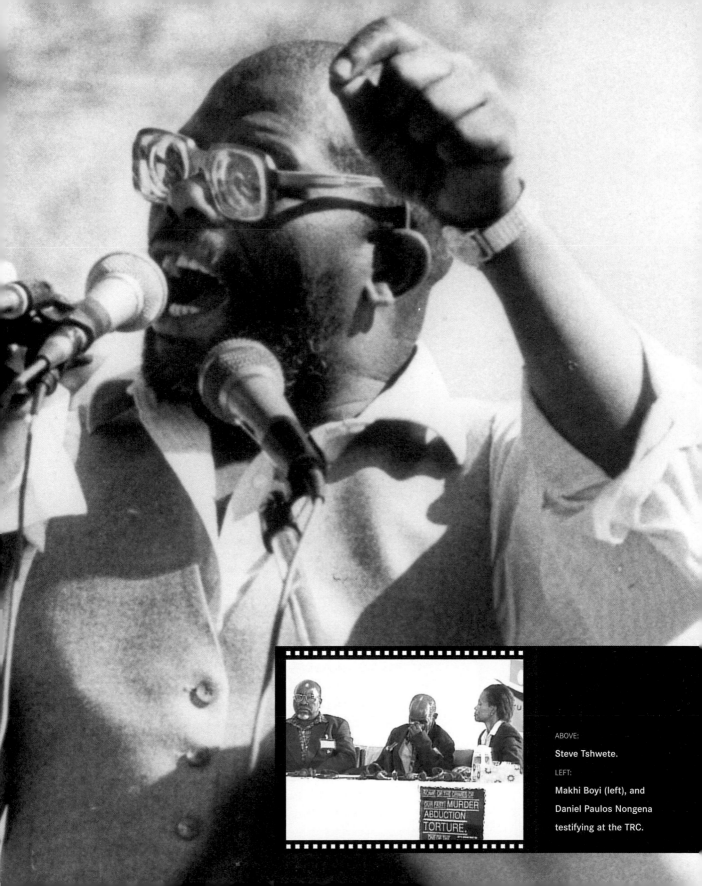

ABOVE:

Steve Tshwete.

LEFT:

Makhi Boyi (left), and
Daniel Paulos Nongena
testifying at the TRC.

6. GWENTSHE, Mzimkulu

7. GWENTSHE, Mziwandile David

8. KONDILE, Tumbekile Edward

9. KONDOTI, Malcomess Johnson

10. KONDOTI, Miriam Montshake

11. MABONA, William Galelekile

12. MAFU, Best

13. MALOBOLA, Binga British

14. MANDLA, Fezile

15. MANDLA, Mzwandile

16. MARAWU, Zwelinzima Abraham

17. MASONDO, A.M.L.

18. MAZWAYI, Kapi Archi

19. MBEKWA, Ndumiso Albert

20. MBIDLANA, Mafuya

21. MDEMKE, Mangamso Shadow

22. MKINGI, Gloria

23. MJO, Brian Zola

24. MJO, Mzwandile Cyril

25. MJO, Temba Stanley

26. MKUNGWANA, Monde Colin

27. MNIKI, Zulu Edmund

28. MNYUTE, Ndiko John

29. MPAHLAZA, Kubile

30. MPONDA, Wawini Samson

31. MUGQIKAMA, Mncedisi Lyttleton

32. NGAPA, Sijo Giceon

33. NDINGAYE, Velile Bethwell

34. NGQOLA, Sondwabo Sidwell

35. NKANGANA, Buyiselo Bernard

36. NKANYUZA, Gladstone Monde

37. NTLEBI, Malgad

38. ONDALE, Mlambi William

39. PANYANA, Mongesi Effort

40. RALANE, Mbozi Eric

41. SAKWE, Lungele Rhodes

Extract from list of co-conspirators, Rivonia Trial.

Several of the surviving Rivonia Trial co-conspirators came forward to testify against Card. On 23 July 1996, Mfene Simon Yoyo testified that he had been tortured by Card in 1963, the year in which so many individuals had admitted to Card that they were members of the ANC. Card denied the claim. On 14 May 1997, Makhi Boyi and Daniel Paulos Nongena testified that they, too, were tortured and threatened with death by Card in an effort to extract a confession from them. Card denied the charge, indicating that he was well known in the area for his policing of political matters, and it was these activities that led to his name being attached to many events in which he had no involvement.

On 11 June 1997, Zweliyazuza Gwentshe testified that Card had perpetrated atrocities on the Gwentshe family and that his brother Mzwandile had been tortured by Card. In a written submission to the TRC, Card again denied the allegation, pointing out that after Mzwandile's other brother, arrested at the same time, was released, Card and that brother had become good friends. 'We actually visited each other at our respective homes and there was never a suggestion that the family was bearing a grudge.' On the same day, Vuyani Mngaza testified before the TRC that he had been tortured by Card. Again, in a written submission to the Commission, Card denied the allegation. Then, on 13 June 1997, Mncedisi Mapela testified that he had been taken from Maziza's tailor shop where he worked, and tortured by Card and two others. In a written response to the Commission, Card confirmed his involvement in an investigation of Maziza, but claimed that Mapela, if he identified him correctly, had agreed to supply him with information. He denied assaulting Mapela.

On 9 August 1998, the remains of Washington Bongco were reburied at his Fort Beaufort home in a formal commemorative ceremony. Bongco was the first head of the Border Region of the armed wing of the ANC, convicted of political offences and hanged on 10 December 1964. The evidence given by Card at his trial was pivotal in sending him to the gallows.

The official biography prepared for the commemorative event noted that he was severely tortured by Card during a 90-day detention period. *Dispatch Online* reported that speaker after speaker at the memorial ceremony claimed that Card harassed and tortured political activists during his days as a security policeman in East London. Steve Tshwete, by this time the national Minister of Sport, related in his speech that, under torture, Bongco agreed to be Card's informer as a ploy to set up a trap to kill Card, a trap that Card ultimately evaded. Beyond the allegations of torture – and not covered by the TRC hearings – is the role played by Card in ensuring long sentences for Eastern Cape ANC members. The Security Police, in collaboration with the apartheid legal system, devised ways of splitting the single offence of being a member of the ANC into a number of separate offences – for example, recruiting members, and propagating the aims and objectives of the organisation. This frequently resulted in the accused receiving multiple sentences.

On 14 May 1997, the local TRC Chairperson asked in session: 'Who is Donald Card? ... [On] the one hand there is the picture of Donald Card, the man who lays his life on the line, sacrificing all in order to take that fateful step of assisting Donald Woods into exile ... Donald Card who we have to respect and admire, to salute for tremendous courage. Then there is on the other hand this other picture of Donald Card, if you can excuse my words ... Donald Card the monster who terrorised freedom fighters in this area. Old peasant men who were trying to make a statement about the need for democracy in our country ... placed under terrible conditions by that Donald Card.'

The Commission posed the conundrum, but could not resolve it. The archival threads around Donald Card are knotted indeed.

The archive laid down in the pages of the Daily Dispatch, in the TRC process, and in the countless memories that survive, enters an enigmatic dialogue with the Rivonia Trial transcript almost 40 years earlier, and the handover ceremony at the Nelson Mandela Foundation in 2004. The glimpses of the records reproduced here give us a taste of the many interpretations they afford and the likely preoccupations of researchers for years to come. The archive, which contains countless other slivers pertaining to Card, associated events and persons, holds open such questions for continuous review. Such review is central to the call of justice.

By his own account, Card made a number of attempts to return the two old notebooks to their owner after Mandela's release. It was only when the Centre of Memory was established in 2004 that Card was finally able to realise this goal. The story of the notebooks draws attention to the role of the Centre in calling out the texts of the archive from the many unknown places where they have been lodged over the years. In his speech made at the opening of the Centre of Memory, Mandela characterised the notebooks as representing the hope of recovering memories and stories suppressed by the apartheid regime, as well as securing the surprisingly elusive official records of the period.

The act of reconciliation at the opening event is shown, through the revelations made by studying the archives, to go to the heart of apartheid violence and struggle, histories of death and attempted killings, the workings of an extensive security apparatus, political transition and the making of democracy. It reveals sharply the way in which so many archival records that apparently centre around the figure of Nelson Mandela are not confined to the man himself. It raises forcefully the power of secrecy and the potential for liberation that a commitment to opening archives brings to all.

Ahmed Kathrada (left), Mandela and Donald Card with the Centre of Memory Project team at the Nelson Mandela Foundation, September 2004.

Mandela at the
exhibition launch.
OVERLEAF:
The exhibition at the
Constitutional Court.

1987   It's sunny today in South Africa

THESE ARE MANDELA'S PERSONAL DIARIES FROM 1976 TO 1989, ORDERED
FROM JUTA'S STATIONERS. IN THEM, MANDELA ENTERED A WIDE RANGE
OF INFORMATION: LETTERS WRITTEN AND RECEIVED, TIMES AND
DURATION OF VISITS, HIS STATE OF HEALTH, IMPORTANT POLITICAL EVENTS
IN SOUTH AFRICA AND ABROAD, FILMS HE WATCHED, BOOKS HE READ,
THE NATURE AND LENGTH OF HIS LEGAL CONSULTATIONS, HIS APPEALS
TO THE AUTHORITIES – AND THE DREAMS HE HAD AT NIGHT.

SOUTH AFRICA TODAY

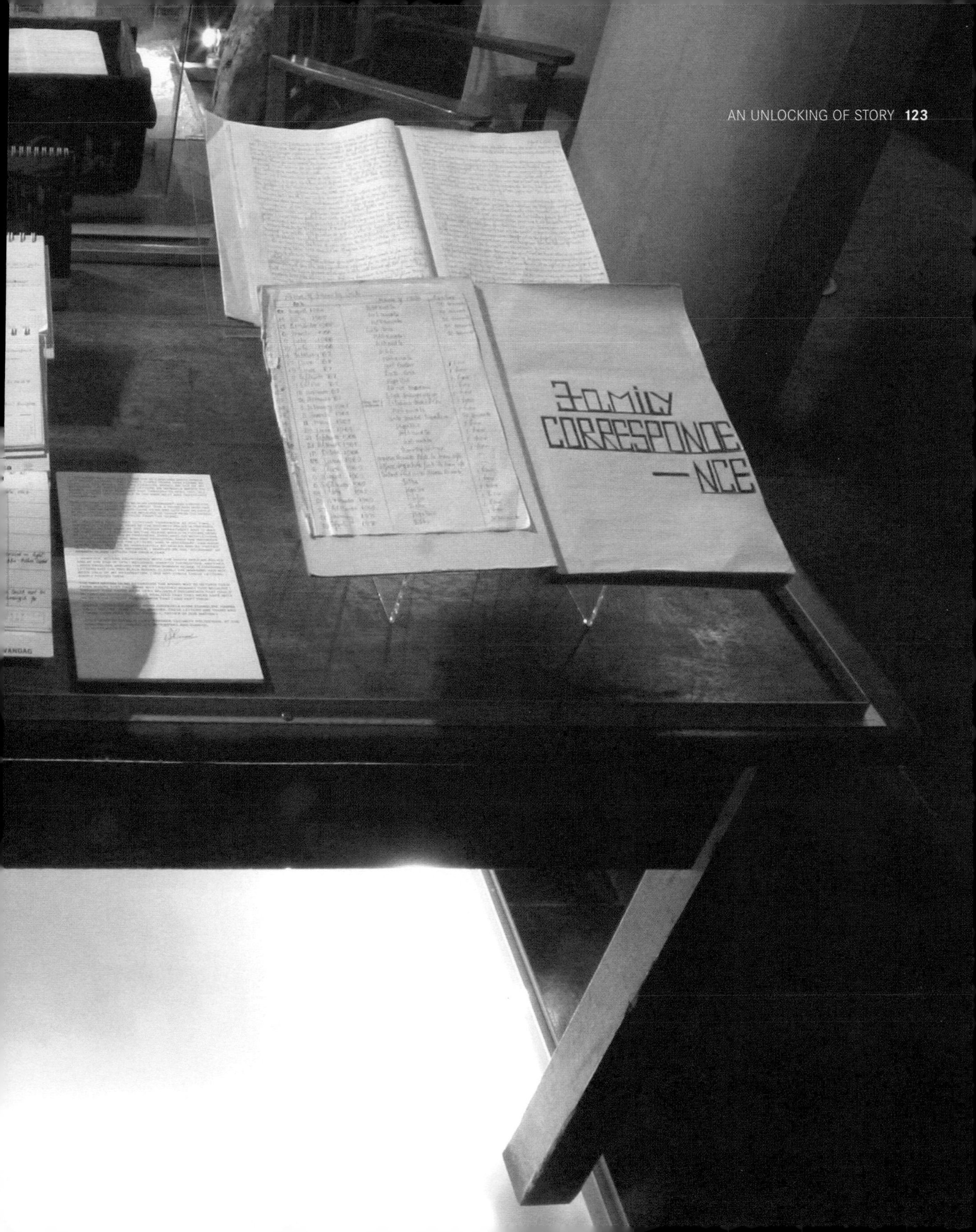
Family
CORRESPONDE
—NCE

A Closer Reading
Exhibiting the Prison Archive

The Centre of Memory's first act in presenting the Prison Archive was the 2004 exhibition 466/64: A Prisoner Working in the Garden, initially displayed at the Nelson Mandela Foundation and then in the foyer of the South African Constitutional Court in Johannesburg. The long-lost images of Nelson Mandela in the prison 'garden' in 1977 triggered the theme of the exhibition as they revealed a portrait of Mandela that had been largely unexplored: indignant, defiant, proud and angry. The exhibition followed a series of archival threads that emerged from those forgotten photographic images: records of defiance, challenge, negotiation and dialogue; of personal emotions of anger, grief and love; and the tangles of the personal and the political. The exhibition was not based on a systematic review of the Prison Archive. In fact, the 76 boxes in the National Archives, accompanied by only a rudimentary inventory, make systematic investigation difficult and this is especially true when – as is almost always the case – one document leads to another. The exhibition was, instead, something of a chance encounter with the prisoner through the archive, in the course of which a number of records leapt out at the exhibition researchers.

The compilers of the exhibition constantly faced the question of how much of the private man to reveal – voyeurism is, of course, the eternal temptation of archivists – and elected to err on the side of discretion, recognising that discretion is its own kind of censorship. But the discretion was not confined to the figure of Mandela. In the quest to understand better one of the most famous people in the world, questions remain about the rights of sons, daughters and friends. Sensitivities borne out of ongoing controversies also required attention and, in some instances, affected the choice of documents for exhibition. The exhibition signalled its choices by allowing certain excluded materials to peep out from under the selected ones, alerting the viewer to their presence and to the exertion of curatorial selection.

Where previously the official Prison Archive had been consulted by a biographer in order to narrate the story of Mandela's life, the exhibition sought rather to confront the physical traces of the prison experience. The makers of the exhibition invited viewers to engage with the objects themselves, and to think about what they might mean.

466/64 A Prisoner Working in the Garden

The exhibition was structured as a spatial metaphor for incarceration, premised on the idea of an island prison, where the prisoner was not simply confined by bars but isolated from the world by the sea, and by multiple systems of censorship, intervention, secrecy and lies. The self-contained exhibition had clearly delimited boundaries, and visitors were obliged to step – quite literally – into the prison world. Their entry was signalled by the sound of gravel crunching underfoot, evocative of the island and the limestone quarry. The enclosing steel mesh screens suggested the cell and its cold isolation, and yet, because the screens also allowed visual access, they also signalled the failure of the prison system to contain the spirit of the prisoners.

A centrally placed desk at the entrance marked bureaucratic regulation of the prison experience. The stacks of metal trunks and wooden crates in which many of the documents were exhibited conveyed a sense of the mass of heaped records, and evoked their crated passage to and from Robben Island.

Their new glass lids, designed to enable viewing, symbolised their latter-day transition into the public domain and their new accessibility.

Certain documents were placed in display cabinets, introducing the idea of engagement with the archive. Their multiple drawers invited viewers to interact with the display, to open and close the archive as they wished. Glass boxes elevated the principal objects of the exhibition, such as the photographic images of the 'prisoner in the garden'. Flickering video footage, audio, and the veiled space of the world beyond the mesh all generated a sense of uneasiness that was haunting, and evocative of the defiance and anger in the central images of Mandela as the prisoner in the garden. The exhibition itself enabled a powerful, visceral engagement with the archive.

Reading the Prison Archive

The interaction between a reader and the documents of the archive is quite different from the relationship between a viewer and the objects on display at the exhibition. But, just as the exhibition invited the viewer to interact with the display, so too this book, and its presentation of the Prison Archive, invites active reading.

This volume does not try to simply reproduce the exhibits. Instead, it focuses on three themes at the heart of the exhibition: Mandela and his captors, Mandela's inner world, and Mandela and the world beyond the prison. The documents uncovered on these pages are open to countless rereadings and reinterpretation as the reader's view of the archive itself shifts and changes, or as the reader returns to the archive, after a time, with new questions and new understandings. Like the exhibition itself, this chapter presents a partial view of the Prison Archive, as any presentation always is. As such, it is but an invitation into the wider archive.

Mandela and his captors

The Prison Archive is essentially a record of the complex negotiation of power between Nelson Mandela and his captors, a relationship that shifted over time. This relationship is captured primarily in the vast number of letters by Mandela to a variety of authorities concerned with the incarceration, and in their responses to him.

In the early years of his sentence, the Prison Archive reveals, Mandela emerged as the elected spokesperson of the prisoners and, as such, kept a record of his interventions that was every bit as meticulous as those of the prison authorities themselves. In fact, his letters to the authorities began to define the relationship between them and the prisoners, insisting on principles of conduct for both parties.

Where the prison sought, through a system of punishment and privilege, to induce prisoners to discipline themselves in line with the requirements imposed by the regime, the prisoners persistently challenged the moral foundations of that regime and elected rather to discipline themselves in terms of their own code. They steadfastly refused to internalise the norms of the prison system. So, where the prison defined them as criminals, they insisted on their status as political prisoners and judged the system for its moral failure.

466/64 Nelson Mandela.   Speciale brief na BO.

1 + 3.

Bygb   Annexure A.

VERTROULIK
CONFIDENTIAL

Robben Island.
12 July 1976.

The Commanding Officer,
Robben Island.

Attention: Col. Roelofse.

The attached letter is for the personal attention of the Commissioner of Prisons General Du Preez, and I should be pleased if you would approve and forward it to him.

I am putting it in a sealed envelope addressed to you and marked "Confidential and for the personal attention of Col. Roelofse." But once I hand it over to the official in charge of the Section, I have no further control over it and cannot guarantee that it will reach you in the condition in which it left me.

NRMandela.

Robben Island.
12 July 1976.

The Commissioner of Prisons.
Pretoria.

<u>Attention: General Du Preez.</u>

I must draw your attention to the abuse of authority, political persecution and other irregularities that are being committed by the Commanding Officer of this prison and members of his staff. Although this letter raises complaints of a personal nature, some of them affect other prisoners as well and it may, therefore, be necessary to mention certain names by way of illustration of these irregularities.

During the last 14 years of my incarceration I have tried to the best of my ability to cooperate with all officials, from the Commissioner of Prisons to the Section warder, as long as that cooperation did not compromise my principles. I have never regarded any man as my superior, either in my life outside or inside prison, and have freely offered this cooperation in the belief that to do so would promote harmonious relations between prisoners and warders and contribute to the general welfare of us all. My respect for human beings is based, not on the colour of a man's skin nor authority he may wield, but purely on merit.

Although I did not agree with the approach of General Steyn on the country's major problems and the policy of the Department of Prisons, nevertheless, respected him as head of this department and as an individual and have never had occasion to question his integrity. Even though I think he could have done more than he did to promote the welfare of prisoners here and elsewhere in the country, his genial and unassuming manner made it easy for me to discuss with him otherwise delicate matters and, in spite of many disagreements I had with him from time to time on the actual decisions he made on specific issues, he was often prepared to give a reasoned motivation for his actions.

I met your immediate predecessor, Gen. Nel, when he came to the island in 1970 with Mr Dennis Healey and, bearing in mind the few remarks we exchanged on that occasion, I have no reason to think that as head of this Department he fell short of the standard set by his

/ predecessor

G.P.-S. (M-S)

DEPARTEMENT VAN GEVANGENISSE
PRISONS DEPARTMENT

Telegrafiese adres:
Telegraphic address: "Gevangenisse"

G.128

VERTROULIK
CONFIDENTIAL

The Officer Commanding

Prison Command

Private Bag ROBBEN ISLAND
7400

FOR ATTENTION : SECURITY

The Commissioner of Prisons
Private Bag X136
PRETORIA
0001

U verwysing .... 19......
Your reference

My verwysing **Serial No. 27/7/.76**
My reference   **913**

Telefoon .... **11** .... Uitbr. **2** ......
Telephone   Ext.

SERIAL NO. 913 : NELSON MANDELA : LETTER OF COMPLAINT
TO THE COMMISSIONER OF PRISONS

1. Attached please find a copy of a letter of complaint
    dated the 12th July, 1976 by the abovementioned
    prisoner addressed to the Commissioner of Prisons –
    annexure A.

2-1. BACKGROUND
    Nelson Mandela considers himself as the leader of the
    prisoners on Robben Island and to retain and improve
    this image amongst his fellow prisoners he, from time
    to time, acts as the mouthpiece of the prisoners, by
    raising the so-called general complaints directly to
    the Commissioner of Prisons or the Honourable Minister –
    the highest authority possible.

2-2. Official records are kept of the complaints and requests
    by prisoners and the way of disposal and I am quite
    satisfied that the head of the prison sees them daily
    and that we comply with the provisions as laid down
    in Regulation 103.

                                    2/......

The prisoners did not only challenge the disciplinary regime; they also developed an education system of their own, encapsulated in their idea of Robben Island as their university. They placed a high value on academia, from basic literacy through to higher degrees, and studied either among themselves or through outside institutions. In this way, they turned their place of incarceration into a place of learning, and thus challenged the ability of the prison system to humiliate them. The increasingly thwarted authorities responded by turning study regulations into a primary instrument of discipline – thereby, of course, surrendering their own moral claim on the idea of prison as rehabilitation. The Prisons Commissioner reserved 'the right to suspend studies at any time should he deem it necessary or for some other reason'.

Hundreds of papers and cards related to the prisoners' campaigns for study rights have survived and it is clear that the prisoners had to go to battle around every aspect of their studies, from the ordering of pens and exercise books, to the right to have reading lights at night, prescribed reading glasses, and other study materials. Mandela wrote many letters requesting assistance from friends at home and abroad. He also wrote countless appeals to the authorities, contesting petty regulations like not being allowed to receive books for courses that were recommended but not prescribed.

At this time, Mandela was also campaigning for the authorities to adhere to the rules of prison communication. By the mid-1970s Mandela's approach was sterner, sometimes angry and indignant, as seen in the 1977 photographs of the 'prisoner in the garden'. He used his legal training to register his displeasure and assert the prisoners' rights on Robben Island. Conditions on the island were harsh, particularly in the early years. But the situation improved significantly as a result of protests by Mandela and other prisoners as well as official visits to the prison by high-profile figures such Helen Suzman, sole voice of dissent in the South African Parliament, and the International Committee of the Red Cross. By 1978 B-section prisoners were no longer required to do hard labour, and from 1980 the prisoners were allowed access to newspapers. Conditions at Pollsmoor were better, but in 1985 Mandela was still petitioning for their right to be treated as political prisoners.

Mandela also engaged officialdom on the matter of his personal circumstances, particularly when the actions of the state affected his family. Despite being cut off from all his relatives, Mandela felt a great sense of responsibility for their wellbeing. He was particularly concerned about his wife and their children as they were constantly harassed by the police. Winnie was first forbidden from leaving Johannesburg and was later held in solitary confinement before being banished to Brandfort. Mandela had been married to her for only four years before he was imprisoned, and he felt partly to blame for the hardships she endured.

OPPOSITE:

Extract from letter of complaint by Mandela about censorship of correspondence.

"But if you really want to be in top condition for such strenuous games as rugby, which require tremendous reserves of energy and speed, you'll have to pay due attention to your diet — eat well, I repeat, eat well! though I do not know where mum will raise all the cash for that."

The passage was disallowed and Lt-Prins refused to give me any explanation about the matter.

As my grandniece, Noliswa Matanzima, wishes to study LL.B with a view of practising as a lawyer and the parents asked for my advice as to whether it would be wise for her to do law. On April 15 I wrote back to them encouraging my grandniece to proceed as she wished, but at the same time advised the parents that I have been out of practice for 16 years and would accordingly consult Mrs I. Kentridge, who formerly practised at the Johannesburg Bar. On May 9 I wrote to Mrs Kentridge along the lines indicated above and, on June 4, Lt Prins arrogantly told me that I should re-write the letter and leave out the facts mentioned above, adding that the Matanzimas could get the advice from somebody else.

It was the hostility with which he spoke more than his unreasonable ~~attitude~~ explanation that struck me. In addition, I wondered what had happened to my letter of April 15. Whatever they did with it they acted improperly. If they sent it to the Matanzimas then they allowed me to make a promise to my relatives which they knew in advance ~~that~~ they would not permit me to fulfil. If the letter was held back, I should have been told about the matter, which was not done.

To prevent me from telling my ~~daughter~~ wife that I sent my daughter a birthday card which did not reach her, that I always think of her and that the photos she had posted to me had disappeared is an unreasonable act based neither on security considerations nor on the desire to maintain good order and discipline nor to promote my welfare. The same applies to my letter to Mrs ~~Kentridge~~ in which I requested her to advise my grandniece on her desire to become a lawyer.

Censorship of Incoming Correspondence

But the worst abuses in regard to the censoring of letters are committed in regard to incoming correspondence and, in this connection, the C.O. and his staff have gone rampant. The censoring is malicious and / vindictive...

As a result, he made constant appeals to the authorities around his domestic affairs. The authorities often took months to respond and, more often than not, turned down his requests.

On 13 May 1974, an anxious Mandela wrote to the Minister of Justice, Jimmy Kruger, about repeated attacks on his family and home in Soweto. 'I am quite certain that if you think that my representations are reasonable and substantial, and you consider it your duty to help, all red tape will be brushed aside and our problems could be solved with a stroke of the pen.'

Mandela approached the Minister in a manner that assumed the latter would share his concern about a woman living alone in a house, under threat. He was, of course, all too well aware that Kruger was the same Minister who had confined his wife, in terms of the provisions of the 1950 Suppression of Communism Act, to living in Orlando township, thereby making her vulnerable to attack. His requests for her to be given adequate protection were equally cognisant of how readily such requests would have been treated if the safety of a white woman was at stake. The framing of the appeal in terms of a shared humanity constituted a profound critique of apartheid. In his letter, Mandela quoted his earlier letter on the same subject to the Minister's predecessor:

I cannot get myself to accept that you could remain indifferent where the very life of another human being is involved.

But Mandela did not only ask the Minister to empathise with his situation and that of his wife. He, in turn, explicitly placed himself in the Minister's position:

I am well aware that, in view of all the circumstances, my representations will have to be approached cautiously and carefully, and that a decision either way will carry a heavy responsibility. Your official capacity may demand that you should pay attention to policy and security considerations which will result in grave injustice to specific individuals. I am also aware that the decisions you arrive at in your ministerial capacity may frequently clash with your personal feelings in matters of this nature... Above all, is the fact that the central issue in this matter is that the life of another human being, of a citizen, is at stake. I feel confident that in examining my requests you will allow humanitarian considerations to override all others, and do everything in your power to enable my wife to lead at last a normal and happy life.

OPPOSITE:
Extract from letter to
Minister of Justice,
13 May 1974.

(Nelson Mandela to Minister of Justice, 13 May 1974)

10. Inspite of all her bitter experiences my wife has no intention whatsoever of leaving the house. But I think it advisable for her to be furnished with a passport to enable her to travel abroad on holiday. Getting away from Orlando for a month or two might ease the strain and benefit her health immensely.

11. I must add that although I have now completed eleven years of my sentence, and although I have reached "A" Group, the highest classification a prisoner may attain, I have never been given the privilege of a contact visit with my wife. I have been forced to discuss serious domestic problems across a glass partition, and under difficult conditions where I have to shout to be heard even in regard to highly confidential matters. Moreover, the one hour allocated for the visit is too short a period, if account is taken of our special problems. I must accordingly ask you to allow me a two hour contact visit, with all the normal liberties and courtesies associated with such visits, for the purpose of discussing these special problems.

12. I am quite certain that if you think that my representations are reasonable and substantial, and you consider it your duty to help, all red-tape will be brushed aside and our problems could be solved with a stroke of the pen.

13. It would be quite easy for you to reject each and every one of the requests I have made. You could, for example, point out that the question of the relaxation of influx control regulations is a matter outside your competence and within the jurisdiction of the Johannesburg City Council. You could adopt the same attitude towards my request in regard to the South African Police and passports, and tell me that my wife and I should apply directly to the appropriate authorities. You could even go further to rub it in by adding that my wife, in fighting racial oppression, has deliberately invited all the troubles she is now experiencing, and that the Security Police, in giving more than ordinary attention to her movements and activities, are carrying out their normal duties under the law.

14. I am well aware that, in view of all the circumstances, my representations will have to be approached cautiously and carefully,

5/.....

-5-

and that a decision either way will carry a heavy responsibility. Your official capacity may demand that you should pay attention to policy and security considerations which will result in grave injustice to specific individuals. I am also aware that the decisions you arrive at in your ministerial capacity may frequently clash with your own personal feelings in matters of this nature.

15. The representations contained in this letter are made in the knowledge and certainty that they can be approved in such manner and under such conditions as will not endanger the security of the State or the public interest.

Above all, is the fact that the central issue in this matter is that the life of another human being, of a citizen, is at stake. I feel confident that in examining my requests you will allow humanitarian considerations to override all others, and do everything in your power to enable my wife to lead at last a normal and happy life.

Yours faithfully,

(Signed) N. Mandela
NELSON MANDELA 466/64

Mandela asked that the matter be treated as 'one of utmost urgency'. But more than a year later he was still petitioning for the issues to be dealt with. On 16 February 1975, the authorities dealt with just one of the six issues raised by Mandela, refusing permission for his brother-in-law to reside with Winnie. Not satisfied with the authorities' response, he again – on 11 September 1975 – sought permission to write to Prime Minister John Vorster about his 'household affairs'. The request was turned down on 11 May 1976, two years after his original petition, and the matter declared closed by the prison authorities. 'Red tape' and delays were apparently the only strategy the authorities could muster in the face of this crafted, principled appeal that denied the very rationale of the imprisonment – the idea that 'blacks' were subjects of the regime, while 'whites' were citizens. The Minister, rather than the prisoner, is being asked to consider whether his behaviour is reasonable.

In response to the 1977 media propaganda visit organised by the state, Mandela and his fellow prisoners sent a strongly worded letter to the prison authorities protesting the visit of the journalists.

Mandela's polite but commanding tone makes letters such as these read more like reports from an official than requests from a prisoner. His assumption of a voice of authority was underpinned by his deployment of legal expertise, an insistence that the authorities adhere to their own rules and procedures and a respect for order. Some of the letters were written in Afrikaans, which he studied while in prison. Mandela typically used his letters to lay down a meticulous paper trail regarding conditions, complaints, abuses and requests. They were all unwavering in their adherence to principle and often challenged the officials to confront their consciences. In their every manoeuvre, the letters denied moral authority to the captors while, at the same time, offering them the opportunity to respond with humanity.

While the more militant prisoners on the Island believed that Mandela's attitude to the authorities was, at times, too accommodating, the letters nevertheless infuriated and disconcerted the officials. As early as 1969, when an earthquake had shaken Robben Island as well as the Cape mainland, Mandela had written to the Commissioner of Prisons drawing attention to the absence of safety procedures on the Island. The official response was, even then, irritable and resentful of the authority given to Mandela by the prisoners. In July 1976, Mandela addressed a 25-page complaint to the Commissioner of Prisons in Pretoria, detailing abuses of authority by the warders, their interference in social relations, issues around censorship and the control of visits, health problems and acts of victimisation. When asked for his response, the Commanding Officer on the Island recommended that 'Mandela be degraded to a D-Group [the least privileged] ... to ensure that his subversive activities will be eliminated to a certain extent'. The Commissioner, however, rejected the Commanding Officer's proposal.

N/3/75   ①   11 September 1975.

The Commanding Officer,
Robben Island.

Attention: Col. Roelofse

I should like to obtain the permission of the
Commissioner of Prisons to write to the Prime Minister in
connection with my household affairs.

You are aware that on 13 May 1974 I wrote and made
certain representations to the Minister of Justice, Adv. Kruger,
arising out of repeated attacks on my family and house, the
nature of which were set out in the abovementioned letter.
Amongst these representations was the request that my wife's
brother be allowed to enter the urban area of Johannesburg so as to
live with my wife at 8115 Orlando West during my absence from
the house.

All my representations were rejected save the one relating to
my wife's brother, which the minister advised was still under
consideration. On 12 February 1975 I wrote and asked the minister
to reconsider his decision in regard to the question of supplying my
wife with a firearm. I also requested him to give me his decision
in regard to my wife's brother. On 25 March I was informed,
through you, that the original rulings stood. In this way the
minister disposed of my representations in regard to my wife's
brother without accepting or rejecting them. It is now sixteen
months since my original representations were made and,
since my family continues to be subjected to these attacks I
am compelled to ask the Commissioner to allow me to put the
whole matter to the Prime Minister. In this regard I should
like to expedite the application so that my representations could
reach you the Prime Minister before the next attack is launched.

I should further ask you for a special letter to inform
my wife fully of all the attempts I have made so far to bring

FILM TRANSCRIPT:

Deputy Commissioner of Prisons General Jannie Roux on the Robben Island landing strip:
'Well, for well over fifteen years there has been all sorts of allegations made about
Robben Island. It has been called a place which is something like a barren rock.
It's been called the Alcatraz of South Africa. And therefore the Minister ...
the Honourable Minister of Justice is going to issue this: "With reference to the
allegations of bad conditions made from time to time in respect of Robben Island
Prison, I have invited the local and foreign news media to visit Robben Island in
order to ascertain for themselves the true treatment circumstances of the prisoners
incarcerated there for offences against the security of the state."'

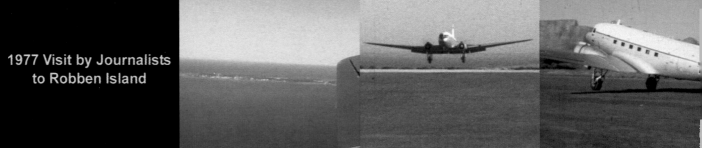

1977 Visit by Journalists to Robben Island

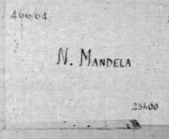

FILM TRANSCRIPT: Outside Mandela's cell

Journalist: (Pointing to the label outside Mandela's prison cell door) **'What is 466 there?'**

General Roux: **'466 – that is his prison number. This** (pointing to the 23h00 number) **has got something to do with his study hours. He's allowed to have late lights until 23:00 hours, for study purposes.'**

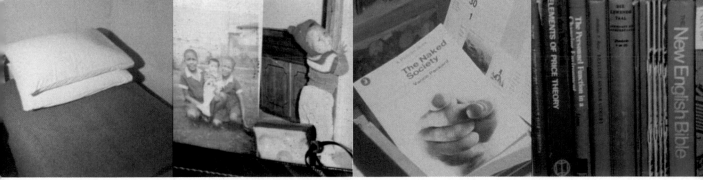

A Pelican Book

The Naked
Society

Vance Packard

The Single Cells Section

ROBBEN ISLAND

19 May 1977

The Head of Prison
ROBBEN ISLAND

We strongly protest against the purpose for and manner in which
the visit to this prison of the local and overseas press and
television men on the 25th April was organised and conducted
by the Department of Prisons. We resent the deliberate viola=
tion of our right of privacy by taking our photographs without
our permission, and regard this as concrete evidence of the con=
tempt with which the Department continues to treat us.

On the 26th April fellow-prisoner Nelson Mandela was informed
by Major Zandberg that the Minister of Prisons had finally agreed
to the repeated requests by the press over the years to visit
Robben Island. We also learnt that the minister had authorised
the visit provided no communication whatsoever would take place
be=tween pressmen and prisoners.

The Minister planned the visit in the hope that it would white=
wash the Prisons Department, pacify public criticism of the De=
partment here and abroad, and counteract any adverse publicity
that might arise in the future. To ensure the success of the
plan we were not given prior notice of the visit, on that parti=
cular day the span from our Section was given the special work
of "gardening" instead of pulling out bamboo from the sea as we
normally do when we go to work. Some 30 litres of milk was
placed at the entrance to our Section, quite obviously to give
the impression that it was all meant for us, whereas in truth
we receive only 6½ litres a day.

Most of us know that a section of the press here and abroad is
sympathetic to our cause, and that they would have preferred to
handle the operation in a dignified manner. Nevertheless, the
Minister's disregard for our feelings has led to the situation
where total strangers are now in possession of photographs and
films of ourselves. The impropriety of the Minister's action is
sharpened by the Department's persistent refusal to allow us to

2/.....

take and send our photographs to our own families.

We stress the fact that the way in which the Minister planned this visit in no way differs from previous ones. IN August 1964 re= porters from "The Daily Telegraph" found those of us who were here at the time "mending clothes" instead of our normal work at the time of knapping stones with 5 lb. hammers. As soon as the re= porters left we were ordered to crush stones as usual. At the end of August 1965 Mrs. I. da Parker from "The Sunday Tribune" found us wearing raincoats on our way back from the lime quarry - raincoats which were hurriedly issued to us at work on the very day of her visit, and which were immediately taken away when she left. The rain coats were not issued to us again until a year or so later.

We emphatically state that under no circumstances are we willing to cooperate with the Department in any manoeuvre on its part to distort the true state of affairs obtaining on this island. With few exceptions our span has been kept inside for several months now, but our normal work is still that of pulling sea-weed, and the Department has given no assurance that we will never be sent out to the quarry again.

We also cite the example of the cupboards we have in our cells. Any television-viewer is likely to be impressed with this furniture and would naturally give all the credit to the Department. It is unlikely that such television-viewers and newspaper readers would be aware that the cupboards have been painstakingly buit with crude tools in a crude "workshop" from cardboard cartons and from driftwood picked up on the beaches by prisoners, that the costs for beautifying them have been borne by the prisoners themselves, and that they have been built by a talented fellow prisoner, Jafta Masemola, working approximately 8 hours a day on weekdays at the rate of R1,50 (One Rand fifty Cents) a month.

At all times wer are willing to have press and television inter= views, provided that the aim is to present to the public a balanced picture of our living conditions. This means that we would be allowed to express our grievances and demands freely, and to make comments whether such comments are favourable or otherwise to the Department.

We are fully aware that the Department desires to protect a favourable

3/......

image to the world of its policies,   We can think of no better
way of doing so than by abolishing all forms of racial discrimi=
nation in the administration by keeping abreast of enlightened
penal reforms, by granting us the status of political prisoners,
and by introducing a non-racial administration through-out the
country's prisons.   With few or no skeletons to hide the Depart=
ment will then no longer stand in any need for resorting to
stratagems.

The actual execution of the plan was entrusted to Gen. Roux and in
his presence, the reporters and cameramen stormed down upon us like
excited visitors to an agricultural show.   From all that we have
seen of Gen. Roux, we are convinced that he has no respect
whatsoever for our feelings and dignity.   The way he handled
the visit is no different from his conduct when he visited this
prison on the 15th November 1976.   On that occasion he conducted
his interviews with us individually in a cloak-and-dagger fashion
in 'the hope of finding us at a complete loss when confronted with
the unrespected.   That there were no ugly incidents as a result
of the provocative action on the 25th April was due solely to our
sense of responsibility.

We are fully aware that we cannot prevent the publication of such
articles on prison conditions here as the Minister might authorize.
But we are equally aware that, whatever the law might be, the
taking of our photographs by the press for publication purposes or
otherwise without our consent, constitutes an invasion of our privacy.
That privacy has been blatantly violated by the very people who,
within the framework of the law, are considered to be its guar=
dians.   And, having violated that privacy, the Department had the
temerity to ask us for permission to make us objects of public
scrutiny.

We stress that we are not chattels of the Prisons Department.   That
we happen to be prisoners in no way detracts from the fact that we
are, nevertheless, South African and Namibian citizens, entitled
to protection against any abuses by the Department.

Finally, we place on record that we cannot tolerate indefinitely any
treatment we consider degrading and provocative and, should the
Minister continue to do so, we reserve to ourselves the right
to take such action as we deem appropriate.

4/.....

F. Anthony
J.E. April
L. Chiba
T.T. Cholo
E.J. Daniels
T.L. Daweti
M.K. Dingake
M.S. Essop
J. Fuzile
K. Hassim
T.H. Ja-Toivo
A.M. Kathrada
N.R. Mandela
J. Masemola
G. Mbeki
R. Mhlaba
K. Mkalipi
W.Z. Mkwayi
A. Mlangeni
E. Motsoaledi
J. Mpanza
P. Mthembu
B. Nair
J.N. Pokela
S. Sijake
W.U. Sisulu
M.M. Siyothula
J.B. Vusani
R.C. Wilcox

happen to be prisoners in no way detracts from the fact that we are, nevertheless, South African and Namibian citizens, entitled to protection
against any abuses by the Department.

Finally, we place on record that we cannot tolerate indefinitely any
treatment we consider degrading and provocative and, should the
Minister continue to do so, we reserve to ourselves the right to take such
action as we deem appropriate.

ANTHONY, F.

APRIL, J. E.

CHIBA, L.

CHOLO, T.T.

DANIELS, E. J.

DAWETI, T. Z.

DINGAKE, M K

ESSOP, M. S.

FUZILE, J.

HASSIM, K.

JA-TOIVO, T H

KATHRADA, A. M.

MANDELA, N. R.

MASEMOLA, J.

MBEKI, G.

MHLABA, R.

MKALIPI, K.

MKWAYI, W. Z.

MLANGENI, A.

MOTSOALEDI, E.

MPANZA, J.

MTHEMBU, P.

NAIR, B.

POKELA, J. N.

SIJAKE, S.

SISULU, W. U.

SIYOTHULA, M. M.

VENKATRATHNAM, S. K.

VUSANI, J. B.

WILCOX, R. C.

Monday
Maandag
Lundi
Montag
25 Journalists, photographers + T.V. representatives visit island + take photographs of prisoner cells building.

Tuesday
Dinsdag
Mardi
Dienstag
26

Wednesday
Woensdag
Mercredi
Mittwoch
27

Thursday
Donderdag
Jeudi
Donnerstag
28

Friday
Vrydag
Vendredi
Freitag
29

Saturday
Saterdag
Samedi
Samstag
30

Sunday
Sondag
Dimanche
Sonntag
1

April
May
Mei

1977

1977   It's sunny today in South Africa

Entry in Mandela's desk calendar detailing the visit by journalists to Robben Island on 25 April 1977.

OPPOSITE:

Final page of original letter of complaint over journalists' visit in Mandela's handwriting.

24 December 1970.

The Commanding Officer,
Robben Island.

Attention : Medical Officer

I should be pleased if you would kindly reconsider your decision
rejecting my application for leave to order 4 lbs of honey per month on
health grounds.

I have been shown your comment on my previous application in
which you stated that I did not need the honey requested. You will
recall that I had earlier shown you a pamphlet of the S.A.B.C. which
contained an address by Dr McGill. I drew your attention to some
paragraph but missed the crucial statement contained in page 5
thereof which I am anxious that you should read.

A perusal of my medical report will reveal that although I have
been put on treatment with a higher potency, and although the rising
of the pressure has been halted, it is far from being normalised. In
reexamining the whole question, I ask you to bear in mind that
applications of this nature raise not only medical issues, but also
those of psychology, etc. I trust that you will give me an opportunity
to discuss the matter ~~again~~ with you again if you consider this second
application inadequate for the purpose of inducing you to reconsider
your decision.

NRMandela.
NELSON MANDELA.

O.C.
The treatment he is on is the best that
modern medicine can provide. Honey is
not a therapeutic substance for hypertension
I therefore refer you to my previous comment
on this matter. I am prepared to see Mandela
at any time to recheck his blood pressure Randolph D/S

Hosp/ ... 24 Desember 1970 ... 28/12/70

Hoof brigadier Van der Berg ...
Hospitaal,
Robben-Eiland. Bar. 12. ...
29/12/70.

Ek sal dit hoog op prys stel as u die twee aangehegte briewe aan die aandag van die geneesheer sal bring.

Ek het afreeds die aangeleentheid van my aansoek vir behuising met u besprek.

NRhnlandela:
NELSON MANDELA: 466/64.

(1) Bev. Ek is nie familie van die Dokter nie. Ek het al herhaaldelik. Kere ... hom gese hy mag nie in brief aan my geadresseer nie et is ... nie die B/ nie.
Quat. Hosp.

Ho. ... D/G ... nota op aansoek.
nie u goedkeuring ...
28/12/70

Mandela's inner world

Insights into the intimate and personal world of the prisoner and his inner workings can be found not only in the two old notebooks, but throughout the Prison Archive. They are perhaps most poignantly expressed in the treasured mementoes that brought human warmth into the small cell he occupied, the thoughts and dreams recorded in his personal desk calendars, and in the love and care, loss and grief expressed in letters to family and friends. Mandela's Robben Island cell has been well documented in a number of photographs, but it is the personal accounts that conjure up the most vivid images of life on the Island.

All of us had one wooden plank for books. For Madiba we built a more extensive shelving around that one plank. Laloo Chiba and I did most of the work, with Michael Dingake and Ahmed Kathrada helping. The extra shelves were made out of two strips of ordinary cardboard, separated by empty matchboxes positioned at strategic points. We then taped the boards together with blue tape, and covered the resulting shelf with plastic sheeting.

(Interview with Mac Maharaj, September 2004)

Mandela's Cell

One envelope in the official Prison Archive contains black-and-white prints, mainly from the 1977 media visit to Robben Island. There are four images of Nelson Mandela's cell (overleaf), which on first inspection were all assumed to have been taken during that visit. However, close scrutiny reveals a more complex scenario. Ahmed Kathrada and Mac Maharaj assisted the Centre of Memory team to interpret them. **Photo 1:** This is the earliest view of Mandela's cell, taken before October 1976 and possibly as early as 1971. The cardboard shelving mentioned by Maharaj is evident, as is the rolled-up bedding under a jacket, and family photographs. **Photo 2:** This is a later view, but predating the 1977 media visit. The wooden lower shelving, hinged doors and flask are visible. Mandela's book collection has grown, but the rolled-up bedding remains in the same corner. **Photo 3:** This image dates from the 1977 media visit, and can also be seen in the SABC footage of the cell. Foregrounded are the *National Geographic* photograph of the 'running woman', the portrait of Winnie, the collection of tomatoes, and the rolled-up blanket on the chair to support Mandela's back. **Photo 4:** Most of the visual evidence in this photograph suggests that it was also taken during the 1977 media visit. The person in the cell appears to be a curious journalist. However, both Kathrada and Maharaj insist that the bed visible in the far-right corner, with two pillows, is not the bed given to Mandela subsequent to Photo 2. The likeliest explanation is that the photograph dates from the 1977 visit, but that the prison authorities had reorganised the cell and deliberately added a luxury feature

1.

2.

3.

4.

Family images are clearly visible in photographs of the cell, as is the picture of an exuberant young woman running. The significance of that particular picture, given as a gift to Mandela by his fellow prisoners, was related at the exhibition and, as a result, was well covered in the media. In response to the coverage, a reader contributed further to Mandela's Prison Archive. In a letter to Mandela, John Moran recounted how, as a white man reading the *National Geographic* in 1975, he would not have given this image a passing glance. He went on to recount his journey of growth out of apartheid-era prejudices, crediting Mandela with an important role in his personal development.

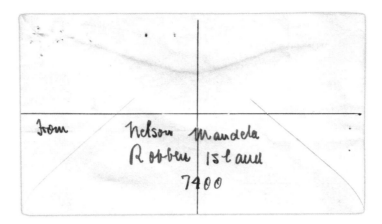

During his incarceration, Mandela wrote hundreds of letters to his immediate family, members of his clan, friends, comrades and admirers. They reveal the many facets of his identity: the loving father, the adoring husband, the stern patriarch, the courtly elder, the dignified statesman, the frustrated prisoner, the confident leader. They also reveal his uncanny ability to remember details about each and every person to whom he wrote.

Mandela longed for more letters, and painstakingly totted up those he received each year. In 1978, for example, he received 43 letters – 15 of them from Winnie. He personally noted that he wrote more letters to women than men, commenting that men 'seem to be totally unaware of the fact that letters were meant to be answered. By comparison, women are more aware of the needs of prisoners.'

In the following extract, Mandela showed his longing to be with his wife Winnie:

OPPOSITE AND OVERLEAF:

**Letter to Winnie signed
Dalibunga, Mandela's
circumcision name.**

By the way the other day I dreamt of you convulsing your entire body with a graceful Hawaiian dance at the BMSC [Bantu Mens Social Club]. I stood at one end of the famous hall with arms outstretched ready to embrace you as you whirled towards me with the enchanting smile that I miss so desperately. I cannot explain why this scene should have been seated at the BMSC. To my recollection we have been there for a dance only once... Anyway the dream for me was a glorious moment. If I must dream in my sleep, please Hawaii for me.
(Nelson Mandela to Winnie, 1 August 1970)

Dade Welsha,   August 1, 1970

Can it be that you did not receive my letter of July 1? How can I explain your strange silence at a time when contact between us has become so vital?

In June I learnt for the first time that you had been confined to bed for 2 months & that your condition was so bad that you did not appear with your friends when the case came up for remand. Is your silence due to a worsening of your health or did the July letter suffer the fate of the 39 monthly letters, letters in lieu of visit & specials that I have written since your arrest on May 12 '69, all of which, save 2, seem not to have reached their destination? Not even Kgatho, Maki, Zeni, Zindzi, Nellie, Ma of Bizana, Marsh & Mashumi responded. I am becoming increasingly uneasy every day. I know you would respond quickly if you heard from me & I fear that you have not done so because you either did not receive the letter or you are not fit to write.

The crop of miseries we have harvested from the heartbreaking frustrations of the last 15 months are not likely to fade away easily from the mind. I feel as if I have been soaked in gall, every part of me, my flesh, bloodstream, bone & soul, so bitter I am to be completely powerless to help you in the rough & fierce ordeals you are going through. What a world of difference to your failing health & to your spirit, darling, to my own anxiety & the strain that I cannot shake off, if only we could meet; if I could be on your side & squeeze you, or if I could but catch a glimpse of your outline through the thick wire netting that would inevitably separate us. Physical suffering is nothing compared to the trampling down of those tender bonds of affection that form the basis of the institution of marriage & the family, that unites man & wife. This is a frightful moment in our life. It is a challenge to cherished beliefs, & putting resolutions to a severe test.

But as long as I still enjoy the privilege of communicating with you, even though it may only exist in form for me & until it is expressly taken away, the records will bear witness to the fact that I tried hard & earnestly to reach you by writing every month. I owe you this duty & nothing will distract me from it. Maybe this line will one day pay handsome dividends. There will always be good men on earth, in all countries, & even here at home. One day we may have on our side the genuine & firm support of an upright & straight forward man, holding high office, who will consider it improper to shrink his duty of protecting the rights & privileges of even his bitter opponents in the battle of ideas that is being fought in our country today; an official who'll have a sufficient sense of justice & fairness to make available to us not only the rights & privileges that the law allows us today, but who will also compensate us for those that have been surreptitiously taken away. In spite of all that has happened I have, throughout the ebb & flow of the tides of fortune in the last 15 months, lived in hope & expectation. Sometimes I even have the belief that this feeling is part & parcel of my self being. It

tons of love + a million kisses. Devotedly, Dalibunga.

Nkosikazi Nobandla Mandela, Central Prison, Pretoria —

Seems to be woven into my very being. I feel my heart pumping hope steadily to every part of my body, warming my blood & pepping up my spirits. I am convinced that floods of personal disaster can never drown a determined revolutionary nor can the cumulus of misery that accompany tragedy suffocate him. To a freedom fighter hope is what a life belt is to a swimmer — a guarantee that one will keep afloat & free from danger. I know, darling, that if riches were to be counted in terms of the tons of hope & sheer courage that nestle in your breast [this idea I got from you] you would certainly be millionaire. Remember this always.

By the way the other day I dreamt of you convulsing your entire body with a graceful Hawaiian dance at the B.M.S.C. I stood at one end of the famous hall with arms outstretched ready to embrace you as you whirled towards me with the enchanting smile that I miss so desperately. I cannot explain why the scene should have been located at the B.M.S.C. To my recollection we have been there for a dance only once — on the night of Lindi's wedding reception. The other occasion was the concert we organised in 1957 when I was courting you, or you me. I am never certain whether I am free to remind you that you took the initiative in this regard. Anyway the dream was for me a glorious moment. If I must dream in my sleep, please Hawaii for me. I like to see you merry & full of life.

I enjoyed reading Fatima's "Portrait of Indian S. Africans" — a vivid description of Indian life written in beautiful & simple style. With characteristic modesty she describes the title in the preface as still pretentious for a book that only skims the surface. But the aspects that form its theme are skilfully probed. She raises an issue of wide interest when she points out that "differences that divide are not differences of custom, of rituals, tradition, but differences of status, of standard of living, of access to power and power-gaining techniques. These are the differences that have at all known times determined the destinies of persons & people, and the same people and the same cultures have at one point enjoyed high privilege and at another none." The book contains chapters which touch on other fundamental matters & I fear that some of her observations on current public questions may spark off animated debates. I welcome the brutal frankness of her pen, but it may be that once she elects to raise such matters her duty is not only to comment but to inspire, to leave her fellow-countrymen with hope & something to live for. I hope you will be able to read the book before the case ends etc. Its a brilliant work written by a brilliant scholar. I thoroughly enjoyed it.

Mr Brown our Cape Town attorney should have been here on July 29 in connection with the question of the guardianship of the children. The sea was very rough & this may probably be the reason for his failure to turn up. I am hoping that he will come soon. In the

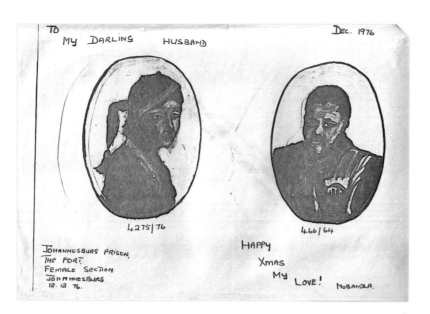

TO
MY DARLING HUSBAND   DEC. 1976

4275/76   466/64

JOHANNESBURG PRISON,
THE FORT,
FEMALE SECTION
JOHANNESBURG
12.12.76.

HAPPY
XMAS
MY LOVE!   NOBANDLA.

Nelson Mandela 466/64 Rewrite   26.11.78
                    1086/78. B

My darling Zindzi,

You don't say whether or not you got my letter of 30/7. Amongst other things, I asked you to send me Oupa's birth date, so that I could also wish him well on such occasions. Please do confirm & let me have the information.

I also got a letter from Zeni, perhaps the best I have received from her for a long time, informative & carefully worded. To anyone who has watched her development from a distance, as I have done, her letters, especially since last yr, showed that her vocabulary & ability to express herself had been a bit affected. But the last letter shows that she is picking up again, & that has really delighted me. When you phone her, please add my congrats.

I am happy to learn that you have taken Mum's advice & that you will now go to the Convent to prepare for your exams. I have already sent you & Oupa my sincerest good wishes. Again I say: "the best of luck." I am confident that you will easily make it.

At Roma there used to be a sister Elizabeth Rhys [sometimes spelt Reyise] from Griquatown. I once asked Mum to find her present address so that I could express our condolences

ABOVE:

Christmas greeting from
Winnie to Mandela.

BELOW:

A letter from Mandela
to his daughter Zindzi
in 1978.

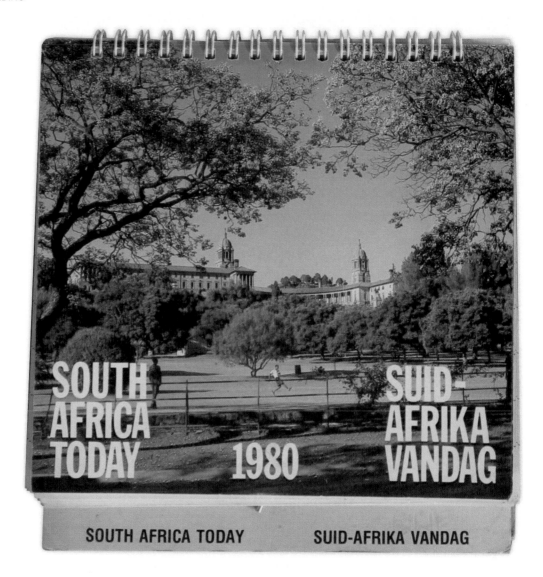

Mandela's personal 'diaries' (more precisely, desk calendars) for the period 1976—1990, ordered from Juta's Stationers, provide a window into his inner world. Donated by him to the Centre of Memory in 2004, they are surprisingly formal and spare. In them, he entered a wide range of information, including letters written and received, important political events in South Africa and abroad, the nature and length of his legal consultations and his appeals to the authorities. He also noted the times and duration of visits, his state of health, the films he had watched, books he had read and the dreams he had had.

Boy initiates of the Southern Ndebele tribe, N. Transvaal. [33] Betty Sonskider. Seuns van die Suidelike Ndebele stam, Noord-Transvaal, word ingewy.

July
Julie
Juillet
Juli
Julio

Sunday / Sondag / Dimanche / Sonntag / Domingo **4**			
Monday / Maandag / Lundi / Montag / Lunes **5**			
Tuesday / Dinsdag / Mardi / Dienstag / Martes **6**			
Wednesday / Woensdag / Mercredi / Mittwoch / Miércoles **7**	Federation of SA Trade Unions (Fosatu) General Workers Union (GWU) & the Food & Canning Workers Union- could see 3 of the biggest emerging Unions - Macwusa & sister Union GWUSA, Had attacked		
Thursday / Donderdag / Jeudi / Donnerstag / Jueves **8**			
Friday / Vrydag / Vendredi / Freitag / Viernes **9**			
Saturday / Saterdag / Samedi / Samstag / Sábado **10**	Zethu, Zimdzi, Zobuhle o Zimbile (Ibo)		

7 | S M T W T F S | S M T W T F S | S M T W T F S | S M T W T F S | S M T W T F S |

SOUTH AFRICA TODAY • **SUID-AFRIKA VANDAG**
Land of Golden Sunshine   Land van Goue Sonskyn

Monday Maandag Lundi Montag	**20**	*Family Day* *Gesinsdag* — Visited by my 4 comrades from women's section of the prison for 2 hrs.
Tuesday Dinsdag Mardi Dienstag	**21**	Birthday card for Maki Weight 73,9.
Wednesday Woensdag Mercredi Mittwoch	**22**	Jim Fish of the BBC announces the resignation of Joe Slovo as MK chief of staff. A comment by John Barratt. Consult Prof. van Rooyen digsberg. Puts additional laser shots on right eye, to see me again in months time.
Thursday Donderdag Jeudi Donnerstag	**23**	Interview with C.O.P. Gen. Willemse, re harassment of family.
Friday Vrydag Vendredi Freitag	**24**	Spend 80 minutes with Rennie. Paid R 40,00 for the laser; requested Bula to fetch her. Given statement to Lt. Col. Maw re Advocate Magid se.
Saturday Saterdag Samedi Samstag	**25**	
Sunday Sondag Dimanche Sonntag	**26**	B.P. 120/89. Pulse 64. Sphygmomanometer (mercurial) 2½ hrs interview with Adv. Alan Magid se. Pentel style pen (royal blue) R4 42.

April
Avril

Photograph: Walter Knirr

Week 17

Luncheon appointments

	March	April	May
Monday	2 9 16 23 30	6 13 20 27	4 11 18 25
Tuesday	3 10 17 24 31	7 14 21 28	5 12 19 26
Wednesday	4 11 18 25	1 8 15 22 29	6 13 20 27
Thursday	5 12 19 26	2 9 16 23 30	7 14 21 **28**
Friday	6 13 20 27	3 10 17 24	1 8 15 22 29
Saturday	7 14 21 28	4 11 18 25	2 9 16 23 30
Sunday	1 8 15 22 29	5 12 19 26	3 10 17 24 **31**

1988

1987   **It's sunny today in South Africa**

Monday Maandag Lundi Montag	**10**	Kruger Day Krugerdag	Weight 73,5 kg. Examined by Dr Stock as usual.
Tuesday Dinsdag Mardi Dienstag	**11**		Examined by Dr Stock as usual.
Wednesday Woensdag Mercredi Mittwoch	**12**		Examined by Dr Stock as usual. Blood specimens taken by Maj. Kleinhans
Thursday Donderdag Jeudi Donnerstag	**13**		Weight 71 kg. Examined by Dr Stock.
Friday Vrydag Vendredi Freitag	**14**		Examined as usual by Dr Stock. Dr Stock returns in the afternoon // Dr Stock visits about 10 p. m.
Saturday Saterdag Samedi Samstag	**15**		Examined by Dr Stock as usual. Examined also by Prof. De Kock. Visited by Zami, Leabie, Zindzi, Zozo & Zondwa.
Sunday Sondag Dimanche Sonntag	**16**		Examined by Dr Stock as usual. Visited by Rev Anthony Sunders.

October
Oktober
Octobre

1988

Photograph: Jean Morris

Week 42

Luncheon appointments

	September	October	November
Monday	5 12 19 26	3 10 17 24 31	7 14 21 28
Tuesday	6 13 20 27	4 11 18 25	1 8 15 22 29
Wednesday	7 14 21 28	5 12 19 26	2 9 16 23 30
Thursday	1 8 15 22 29	6 13 20 27	3 10 17 24
Friday	2 9 16 23 30	7 14 21 28	4 11 18 25
Saturday	3 10 17 24	1 8 15 22 29	5 12 19 26
Sunday	4 11 18 25	2 9 16 23 30	6 13 20 27

1989

1988 **It's sunny today in South Africa**

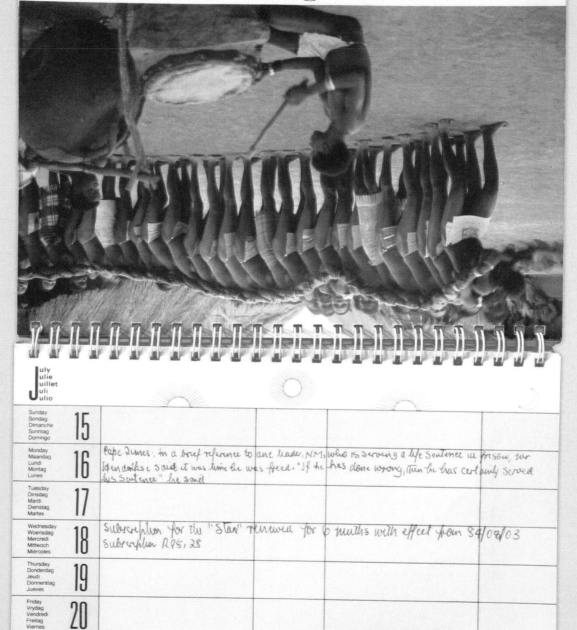

July
Julie
Juillet
Juli
Julio

Sunday Sondag Dimanche Sonntag Domingo	15				
Monday Maandag Lundi Montag Lunes	16	Cape Times: In a brief reference to ane leader, N.M., who is serving a life sentence in prison, mr Hendrickse said it was time he was freed. "If he has done wrong, then he has certainly served his sentence" he said			
Tuesday Dinsdag Mardi Dienstag Martes	17				
Wednesday Woensdag Mercredi Mittwoch Miércoles	18	Subscription for the "Star" renewed for 6 mnths with effect from 84/08/03 Subscription R95, 28			
Thursday Donderdag Jeudi Donnerstag Jueves	19				
Friday Vrydag Vendredi Freitag Viernes	20				
Saturday Saterdag Samedi Samstag Sábado	21				

7

SOUTH AFRICA TODAY
Land of Golden Sunshine

SUID-AFRIKA VANDAG
Land van Goue Sonskyn

Seekant, Durban, met skemer   Sima Eloxson   Durban's Beach Front at dusk

November
November
Novembre
November
Noviembre

Sunday / Sondag / Dimanche / Sonntag / Domingo **28**				
Monday / Maandag / Lundi / Montag / Lunes **29**				
Tuesday / Dinsdag / Mardi / Dienstag / Martes **30**	Indira Gandhi assassinated			
Wednesday / Woensdag / Mercredi / Mittwoch / Miércoles **31**	Bishop Stephen Naidoo (40) appointed as archbishop of C.T. Most Rev. S. Naidoo, Cathedral Place, 12 Boquet St, C.T.			
Thursday / Donderdag / Jeudi / Donnerstag / Jueves **1**	BP $\frac{170}{100}$ taken by sister Du Toit. How the ANC switched to policy of armed struggle: Andrew Prior, Dpt of Political Studies		Cape Times	
Friday / Vrydag / Vendredi / Freitag / Viernes **2**	BP $\frac{190}{110}$			
Saturday / Saterdag / Samedi / Samstag / Sábado **3**	BP $\frac{160}{110}$			

11   S M T W T F S S M T W T F S S M T W T F S S M T W T F S S M T W T F S

Former prison warder
Christo Brand.

The relationship Nelson Mandela developed with warder Christo Brand and his family was one of extraordinary richness. Brand was one of Mandela's warders on Robben Island from 1979, and in 1982 he was transferred to Pollsmoor along with Mandela. In the late 1990s, journalist John Carlin interviewed Brand. Brand's description of Mandela's garden at Pollsmoor is remarkable for the extent to which the warder identified with his prisoner's garden and his prisoner's emotions:

[That was] in Pollsmoor prison. We were fighting for a garden on the top roof. We got these 44-gallon drums cut in half. We brought up some soil, manure and everything … I was also helping him … He and Sisulu were mixing the soil with the manure and filling up the drums. There he started really producing a garden from onions, tomatoes, lettuce and different things he was planting. He was really fond of his garden.

[At Pollsmoor], in the mornings, he woke up early, which we observed through a window … He would first … exercise for at least an hour, push-ups, sit-ups … then he would go to the shower. After that Mandela would come back, start making his bed and things, and carry on with his studies. When we opened at 7:00 … he stood up and he greeted us in the morning … We started dishing out the food … after that he did his washing … Outside were community toilets … and Mandela would do his washing there and would hang up his washing.

He would come back and maybe drink a coffee or a tea ... after he was finished with his garden, he would study there till 12:00 [when] we locked up. Then he was moved back to the community cell ... he would, at least, sleep an hour during lunch hour, wake up at 2:00, exercise outside at the back, walk with his friends, colleagues, walk all around the courtyard, look at his garden before we locked him up. But he would also study.

(http://www.pbs.org/wgbh/pages/frontline/shows/mandela/interviews/brand.html)

Mandela manifested a similar identification with Brand. Early on at Pollsmoor, he wrote to Brand's wife in fluent Afrikaans. The letter and translation are reproduced below. Prisoner and warder stayed in touch after Mandela's release, and in 2000 Mandela even found the time to drop a note to Riaan, one of Brand's children. The record of Mandela's relationship with his warder reveals one of the most striking elements of his Prison Archive: Mandela's countless explorations of, and insistences on, the common humanity of the prisoners and their jailers.

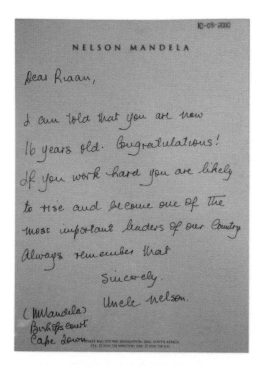

TRANSLATION: **Madam, Your husband is a very talented man with a heart of gold. He is always in a good mood and helpful. But he lacks determination, and consequently neglects his own interests and future, as well as those of his wife and children. On countless occasions I have tried to persuade him to study, but all my attempts have failed completely. I must now request your help. Perhaps you will succeed in getting him to do what other responsible young people across the world do – promote their interests and futures.**

Mandela and the world outside

Although removed from public life, the imprisoned Mandela maintained powerful connections with the wider world, sometimes seeking to influence it directly, and at other times engaging in complex and ongoing discussions. At the same time, however, he and the rest of the leadership in prison took considerable care not to intrude on the authority of the ANC leadership outside. Certain of the letters were formal compositions addressed to the public figures with whom he was acquainted, expressing condolences, congratulations or gratitude, or making requests. In acknowledging contributions and recalling joint actions in the past, many of the letters served to build and maintain networks of support. These contacts with the world outside were variously covert and open.

In 1975 Ahmed Kathrada and Walter Sisulu suggested to Mandela that he write his autobiography. He agreed, and the proposal was presented to the High Organ, a structure set up by prisoners belonging to the ANC and allied organisations in the single cells to organise themselves. Approval was forthcoming and work began on the project. The plan was for the text to be smuggled out of prison by Mac Maharaj when he was released in 1976 and to be published, not only as an inspiration to a new generation of young freedom fighters, but also to draw attention to the ongoing struggle.

Mandela, Kathrada and Maharaj have all recorded their recollections of how the text came to be written in secret and then smuggled off Robben Island. Not unexpectedly, their accounts differ in certain respects, but access to the prison files has contributed significantly to removing such discrepancies and in the process has yielded important insights into the thinking of the prison authorities at the time.

In his memoirs, Kathrada recalls how the text was written in secret:

Fragments of the *Long Walk to Freedom* manuscript with handwriting by Mandela, Kathrada and Maharaj.

Chronicling Mandela's life was illegal and dangerous. Discovery would result in harsh collective punishment ... knowledge of it was to be limited to those directly involved. Because most of the writing would have to be done at night, Mandela feigned illness and was excused from the daily work schedule. He slept for a few hours while the cellblock was deserted and wrote deep into the night. As a registered student of Afrikaans, Madiba was allowed to subscribe to the popular weekly magazine *Huisgenoot*, and he made a deal with the night-duty warders. They were not allowed to bring any reading matter to work, and were only too glad to borrow Mandela's magazines in exchange for allowing him to pursue his 'studies' beyond the 11pm curfew.

(Ahmed Kathrada, *Memoirs*, Zebra Press, Cape Town, 2004, page 265)

death sentence for sabotage had been averted, and an appeal
involved the risk of the Appellate division, the country's highest court of
appeal, holding that the death sentence should have been passed,
with tragic consequences to cases. which ~~would have~~ might adversely
affect future cases. → D

There was also great pressure on the Government demanding our release
and it was felt that an appeal would be exploited by them to relieve
the pressure by arguing that they could do nothing about the matter
until the Appeal court had given its decision, an attitude which
would have been appreciated by many Western countries, organisations
and individuals that were applying the pressure at the time. The
~~and is by itself sufficient to explain their action~~
first was a wise decision, in spite of the fact that it may have ~~cost~~ cost
Ahmed Kathrada unnecessary incarceration and Andrew Mlangeni
and Elias Motsoaledi a sentence of life imprisonment which the
appeal court ~~might~~ ~~may~~ have cut down considerably. Subsequent events
have shown that we were mistaken on the second point and 12
years after Rivonia the nats are still insisting that we should
~~fully serve our respective~~ ~~our respective sentences.~~ sentences

Fighting a case and the threat of a capital sentence did not spare us
from pressing political problems, and our time was often divided between legal consultations and discussion of political matters whenever
lawyers were not present.

The future of sabotage activities came up for discussion quite early during
the trial. A large number of leading MK men had been arrested and others
had fled away, although there were some active units that were doing well,
the precautions taken by the enemy had made operations quite difficult.
There was also the view that the continuation of acts of sabotage would
create a dangerous atmosphere for the trial and that a judgment delivered
in the midst of violent explosions in various parts of the country
might easily go to the other extreme and we recommended their
suspension.

The view was also expressed that mere acts of sabotage unaccompa-
nied by armed struggle could never be effective and that their continuation before the actual commencement of guerilla warfare

Mac Maharaj, in his own memoirs, adds further detail on the writing process:

Mandela started writing in January 1976. He wrote an average of 10 to 15 pages a night. Within three months he had completed the task ... First, there is the writing. Mandela will have to write purely from memory. Then there is the secrecy. He cannot indulge in the luxury of keeping notes in his cell. Whatever he writes each night must be out of his hands the next morning. He has no access to reference works. Conditions require that when he sits to write at night he will not have access to what he has already written.

(Mac Maharaj, *Reflections in Prison*, Zebra Press and Robben Island Museum, Cape Town, 2001, page xii)

Interviews with Maharaj, Kathrada and Laloo Chiba in 2004 and 2005 provide further layers of detail. Each morning, Mandela's text was given to Maharaj to transcribe. Thereafter the text circulated between Kathrada and Sisulu for their comments and queries. Once consensus had been reached, changes were made. The original – in Mandela's handwriting, with comments in the margins by Kathrada, Sisulu and Maharaj – was concealed in plastic cocoa containers and buried in the strip of garden in the courtyard.

In the meantime, Chiba had constructed a file with extra-large covers to house a set of statistical maps that Maharaj was using for his studies, and the final version – in minute handwriting on more than 60 sheets of A4 paper – was then concealed within these covers. Certain sheets were concealed in the covers of other notebooks belonging to Maharaj. When Maharaj was removed from Robben Island in October 1976, pending his release in December, he left the Island with his file and notebooks. The concealed manuscript was not discovered by the authorities. Kathrada recalls the following on the fate of the cocoa containers:

Once we knew that the manuscript was in safe hands, we could destroy the originals, but somehow we never got around to it. For almost a year, the canisters had lain undisturbed in the garden.

The rude awakening came when a construction crew moved into the courtyard without warning and started building a wall that would run straight through our patch of garden. The loss of the garden paled into insignificance in the face of the imminent danger of the canisters being unearthed. Not only would we be severely punished, but the authorities would be alerted to the existence of Mandela's strictly unauthorised autobiography.

As early as possible the next day, we went to retrieve the buried treasure but only managed to save a couple of canisters. We couldn't reach the rest.

OPPOSITE:
Notes for *Long Walk to Freedom* manuscript, with a contribution by Kathrada.

① PAC. Perhaps, ignorant of changes in their policy outside, kept on
denying that they had opened doors to white & Indian.
The news of Duncans membership was condemned by them
as untrue & typical "Congress propaganda."

② When we received news ~~cuttings~~ ~~from Evening Post~~ from section
that ~~the~~ OAU had withdrawn its recognition from PAC
(+ that PAC had been expelled from Zambia ??). the PAC
group has condemned it as typical "Congress propaganda".
They thereupon boycotted all news sessions here.
Later, a copy of the Financial Mail arrived,
containing the original of the news item received by
us, they saw it, but did not apologise for their
allegations. Neither did they resume attending news sessions.

③ ST etc & worked with ~~or~~ C.M. formally, even tho they
knew we were mixed. POQ ~~told~~ arrived & condemned
this as contrary to policy. Led to break up of
~~election~~ Committee

④ Nevilles attack on Chief at commemoration.

~~......~~ campaign was let loose by the whites. The National Party came into
power in 1948 ~~using the slogan~~ promising to keep the "Kaffers" in their
places and driving the "Koolies" out of the country. Among
all ~~sections~~ population groups the Nats built up a pretence of the
Indian as some ~~much~~ hideous monster ~~that~~ who ~~had to be~~ threatened
the lives & livelihood of all the people, and ~~the~~ which had to be
destroyed.

For more than 300 years the ~~s~~ whites have also fostered the idea
that the African is a savage, without a history, culture or worthy
aspiration. He has been reduced to life of hardship, frustration,
bitterness and hostility against all those who enjoy better social,
economic & political opportunities than himself.

History seems to have presented just the opportunity the Nats
had been praying for. What could be better than diverting all the
accumulated frustration and anger of the africans away from the real
issues. The Indian had been presented as his main enemy; & they were the weakest
and most accessible victims.

It was no accident that the police force in Durban was not called
out timeously to curb the rioting. ~~For~~ For, prompt action by the police
could have brought the situation under control on the very first night.
It was no accident that ~~some~~ leading white firms especially let their africa
workers off early & provided them with transport to go into Indian areas.
Instances of whites actually egging the african on against the Indian were
widespread. The ~~police~~ authorities intervened ~~only~~ ~~after~~ effectively only after most
damage was done, and then they turned their guns mercilessly against
the africans. The rioting was eventually drowned in a river of blood.

A few months later, Mandela, Sisulu and I were called into a meeting with General Jannie Roux. He officially informed us that part of the manuscript had been retrieved from its hiding place. As punishment, our study privileges would be withdrawn for the duration of our sentences.

(Ahmed Kathrada, *Memoirs*, Zebra Press, Cape Town, 2004, page 266)

The time delay between the discovery of the manuscript and the implementation of the punishment is, as in so many cases in the Prison Archive, a sign of hidden security concerns or procedures that bear deeper investigation. On discovering the hidden manuscript, the authorities initially considered charging the authors, but that would have placed the manuscript in the court record, and hence potentially in the public domain. So, in an effort to suppress it, the prison regulations were altered in December 1977 and the prisoners' study privileges were withdrawn.

The prison authorities called in a handwriting expert to identify the script of three contributors, Mandela, Maharaj and Kathrada. Maharaj had already been released and was out of the country by the time the containers were discovered. Sisulu's handwriting appeared nowhere on the fragments, but some of the comments recorded by Kathrada made it clear that he had been involved.

The arbitrary punishment inflicted on Mandela, Sisulu and Kathrada was designed to endure for the rest of their sentences, but four years later the authorities relented and restored their study privileges. Twenty-eight years on, the smuggled manuscript eventually formed the basis of Mandela's autobiography *Long Walk to Freedom*, published in 1994.

In an interview in 2005, Maharaj detailed what had happened to the manuscript once it left Robben Island:

OPPOSITE:

Fragment of *Long Walk to Freedom* manuscript in Maharaj's minute handwriting.

With the help of Phyllis Naidoo, we arranged for the file in which the manuscript was concealed to be taken to London by a visitor to South Africa, and delivered to Jay Singh, a South African who was teaching in the UK. Jay was sent a message to pass this file to Rusty Bernstein with a request that he keep it extremely safely until he heard fom me. In August 1977 I arrived in London and met with Rusty and Dr Yusuf Dadoo. Rusty produced the file. He had been puzzled by the message he had received, and did not understand the importance of the statistical maps contained in the file. However, because the message was from me, he had decided to keep the file safely. I pried the covers open, and out came the manuscript pages.

[A.7.8]

Oliver Tambo and Dr Dadoo arranged for Sue Rabkin to assist me in typing up the handwritten manuscript. Sue had arrived back in London after her release from prison. The typed version was completed in January 1978. I retained the master copy, and copies were given to Oliver Tambo and Dr Dadoo. The handwritten manuscript was put away in what was safe storage. However, neither Sue nor I can recall where this storage was. Only a few pages of the manuscript have survived in my possession.

In the eighties the typescript was transferred to a computer disk, and I subsequently gave a copy to Madiba.

(Interview with Mac Maharaj, August 2005)

OPPOSITE:

Letter from Mandela to Mangosuthu Buthelezi, rejected by the prison authorities and never sent. Shenge is Buthelezi's clan name.

Many of Mandela's fellow prisoners were opposed to any dealings with Bantustan leaders, believing that they were puppets of the government. But Mandela disagreed, insisting that a line should always be kept open to them. And so, despite political differences, he kept in close and often intimate contact with his nephew Chief Kaiser Matanzima of the Transkei and his former comrade from the ANC Youth League Chief Mangosuthu Buthelezi of KwaZulu. In one letter to Matanzima – who supported the government on the issue of his uncle's imprisonment, believing that Mandela had indeed broken the law – Mandela instructed his nephew not to lobby for his release into the Transkei. And in a letter to Buthelezi, he expressed his distress at the war between Buthelezi's Inkatha and ANC supporters in KwaZulu, and his desire for reconciliation. Buthelezi read the letter publicly at a meeting of the KwaZulu Legislative Assembly in April 1989. Inevitably, it made newspaper headlines, especially as Buthelezi was technically breaking the law by quoting the words of a banned person.

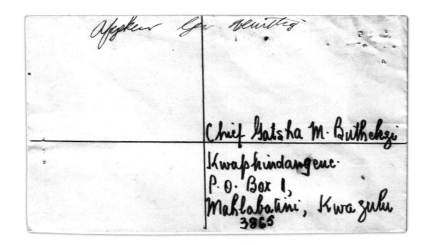

Shenge!

Your unexpected birthday message roused fond memories & made me reflect nostalgically on the multitude of things that mutually interested us. Yrs ago you & I met either in Durban or JHB. & pre-occupied ourselves with warm tête-à-têtes. Each of those occasions left us refreshed & created a greater urge to meet again for rejuvenation.

Eighteen yrs have passed since those good old days & the distance between Mahlabatini & Robben Island became even more magnified through our respective silence. Happily a few govt publications here carried your pictures & those of your family. This usually turned my thoughts to you & MaNdlunkulu Irene. The arrival of your telegram naturally helped to bridge the gap between us.

Thoughts from friends, especially from the old ones, are always a source of strength & inspiration. I should like you to know that I set store by your message. Apart from your telegram I received six other birthday messages, three from the family & three from friends. I treasure all of them & they have given me much comfort. I feel like a 30-yr old. As few as they are, they are representative of all the country's population groups. I believe they form part of the shower of good wishes that have come from far & wide. All of them have given me a shot in the arm. Phungashe!!

2

Recently, I saw films of King Zwelithini's coronation & of his wedding to Princess Mantombi. You led the dancing remarkably well. The scenes reminded me of the beautiful country that straddles i Thukela where part of our history is buried. Unlike the Egyptian Pyramids which attract thousands of tourists every yr from all parts of the globe, Dukuza has vanished & perhaps even the landmarks of the Royal village have been destroyed by all the debris of the 19th & 20th cs. But history will record the proud achievements which issued from the capital of that ancient kingdom, the achievements of Dlangezwa & of NGhungwayo. These names form part of our heritage & are excellent models on which worthy life patterns may be built. When I looked at those films I wondered, as I have done many times in the past, what was so unique in the waters of the Mfolosis as to drive those who drank from it to go through life with such frightening fervour.

Apart from the disappearance of the indigenous states of yore, The S.A. of only 16 yrs ago is no longer the same. The toddlers I left

Letter from Mandela
to Buthelezi,
3 February 1989.

Following his prostate operation in 1985, Mandela was moved into his own spacious cell in Pollsmoor prison. The prison authorities did not divulge the reasons for the separation. When fellow prisoners wished to protest the move, Mandela himself persuaded them to accept it without question. He indicated that good might come out of it. Subsequently, he confirmed that he felt the time was right to start 'talking to the enemy', and that his isolation would facilitate the process. It was from here that he entered into correspondence with the prison authorities and the Minister of Justice, Kobie Coetsee, about 'talks about talks', urging a meeting between the government and the ANC.

Ngubengcuka,

Nobandla has informed me that you have pardoned my nephews, and I am grateful for the gesture. I am more particularly touched when I think of my sisters feeling about the matter and I thank you once more for your kind consideration.

Nobandla also informs me that you have now been able to persuade the Government to release political prisoners, and that you have also consulted with other "homeland" leaders who have given you their full support in the matter. It appears from what she tells me that you and the Government intend that I and some of my colleagues should be released to Umtata.

I perhaps need to remind you that when you first wanted to visit us in 1977 my colleagues and I decided that, because of your position in the implementation of the Bantustan scheme, we could not accede to your request.

Again in February this year when you wanted to come and discuss the question of our release, we reiterated our stand and your plan was not acceded to. In particular, we pointed out that the idea of our release being linked to a Bantustan was totally and utterly unacceptable to us.

While we appreciate your concern over the incarceration of political prisoners, we must point out that your persistence in linking our release with the Bantustans, despite our strong and clearly-expressed opposition to the scheme, is highly disturbing, if not provocative, and we urge you not to continue pursuing a course which will inevitably result in an unpleasant confrontation between you and ourselves.

We will under no circumstances, accept being released to the Transkei or any other Bantustan. You know fully well that we have spent the better part of our lives in prison exactly because we are opposed to the very idea of separate development which makes us foreigners in our own country and which enables the Government to perpetuate our

oppression up to this very day.

I accordingly request you to desist from this explosive plan and we really hope that this is the last time we will ever be pestered with it.

Ozithobileyo,
Dalibunga.

Chief K. Dalwonga Matanzima, Umtata, Transkei.

GEHEIM
SECRET   13 February 1985

The Commissioner of Prisons
PRETORIA

THE SUBJOINED LETTER IS FOR THE ATTENTION OF THE STATE PRESIDENT,
MR   P W   BOTHA :

"The State President,
CAPE TOWN

Sir,

Copies of the Hansard parliamentary record of

25 January to 1 February 1985 were delivered to us on

8 February.

We note that during the debate in the House of Assembly you

indicated that you were prepared to release prisoners in our

particular category provided that we unconditionally renounce

violence as a means of furthering our political objectives.

We have given earnest consideration to your offer but we

regret to inform you that it is not acceptable in its present

form. We hesitate to associate you with a move which, on a

proper analysis, appears to be no more than a shrewed and

calculated attempt to mislead the world into the belief

that you have magnanimously offered us release from prison

which we ourselves have rejected. Coming in the face of such

unprecedented and widespread demand for our release, your

remarks can only be seen as the height of cynical politicking.

We refuse to be party to anything which is really intended to

create division, confusion and uncertainity within the

GEHEIM
SECRET

COMMISSIONER OF PRISONS

In my letter dated 11 September 1989 I have made representations for the
release of certain of my colleagues. I have today been informed that the
Government has decided to approve the release of the following eight colleagues:

      Ahmed Kathrada

      Raymond Mhlaba

      Andrew Mlangeni

      Elias Motsoaledi

      Walter Sisulu

      Wilton Mkwayi

      Jeff Masemola

      Oscar Mpetha.

~~I welcome this constructive move which gives a stamp of credibility to the
address given by the State President on 20 September 1989.~~ *It is my hope* ~~I am confident~~
that their release will contribute to the creation of a climate that will be
conducive to peaceful development and to normalising the situation in our
country. *As previously stated I have not raised the question*
of my release.
~~As is already generally known I am also from my present situation working
for peace and therefor my release is not on the agenda at this stage. I wish
to complete what I have set out to achieve in this regard.~~

                NRMandela
                10. 10. 89.

Mandela found himself in a precarious position. He was aware that by isolating him, the government was playing at divide and rule. But he recognised that, given the escalating crisis in the country, he needed to assume a leadership role, and the government might find it easier to approach him if he were alone. Despite his isolation, Mandela went to great lengths to assure his fellow prisoners and the leaders in exile that he would not commit himself to anything during his secret talks with the government without the ANC's approval. There was, nonetheless, some speculation among comrades outside that he was 'selling out'. Inside Pollsmoor, Walter Sisulu advised caution and Ahmed Kathrada was opposed to the initiative. In a letter from Mandela and his fellow Rivonia trialists to President PW Botha in 1985, they rejected the president's offer to release them if they 'unconditionally renounced violence'. Mandela also prepared a public response to the offer, which was read out by his daughter Zindzi to a packed meeting at Soweto's Jabulani Stadium on 10 February 1985.

In a subsequent memorandum to PW Botha, Mandela responded firmly to the government's insistence that it would only negotiate with the ANC if it renounced violence, broke ties with the South African Communist Party and abandoned its demand for majority rule. Mandela prepared this document from his new residence at the Victor Verster prison – in consultation with his comrades still incarcerated at Pollsmoor – after hundreds of hours of secret talks with the government team. In March 1989 the government accepted this as a preliminary agreement to eventual talks.

Both at Pollsmoor and Victor Verster, Mandela's conversations were bugged by the authorities. Suspecting as much, Mandela and his comrades sought to evade the bugs at Victor Verster by meeting outside under a tree. Little did they know that the tree had also been bugged.

Eventually a secure line – one beyond the reach of the authorities – was set up between Mandela and Oliver Tambo through the intervention of the ANC's Operation Vula. Mandela was increasingly exasperated by Botha's reliance on brute force in response to the continuing crisis in South Africa, and in a letter to the Commissioner of Prisons in March 1989, he voiced his frustration at the government's lack of response to his proposals around talks with the ANC.

During his time at Victor Verster, Mandela was increasingly available to family and friends. He celebrated his 71st birthday with Winnie and 15 other members of the family, including children and grandchildren, as well as with his four colleagues still at Pollsmoor – Sisulu, Kathrada, Raymond Mhlaba and Andrew Mlangeni.

23. 10. 89

22/89

Dear Ndlangisa,

People inside and outside the country rejoice
with you on the return of your beloved Schamela,
and on the lifting of your restrictions. It was
time for him to join you and the family, and it
was time for you both to be free and mobile.

The arrangements for the reception of the seven
comrades were excellent, and their comments at
the press conference beautifully highlighted the
crucial importance of their role in the current
situation. Love and best wishes!

Sincerely,
Madiba

Walter Walter Sisulu

Yeah.

Mrs Albertina Sisulu,
7372 ORLANDO WEST,
P. O. ORLANDO
1804

Letter to Albertina Sisulu,
rejoicing in the release
of her husband Walter.

In a letter to the Commissioner of Prisons on 11 September 1989, he personally requested the release of five of his fellow Rivonia trialists. This matter had been discussed three months earlier, during his first encounter with PW Botha on 5 July 1989, when – although both had agreed on the need for peace – Botha had politely refused Mandela's request to release political prisoners.

In October 1989, however, the government – now under FW de Klerk, who had replaced Botha a month earlier – did indeed release eight political prisoners, including five of the Rivonia trialists, without condition, and Mandela wrote to the families of his fellow trialists, rejoicing in their release.

Then, on 12 December of that year, just after President De Klerk had agreed to his request for a meeting, Mandela sent a memorandum to him, reproduced in full at the end of this chapter. It is an update of the earlier memo written to PW Botha. While welcoming the steps De Klerk had taken since becoming president, the note urged talks with the ANC without preconditions.

8

STAATSPRESIDENTSMINUUT NO:

110

Kragtens die bevoegdheid my verleen by artikel 69(1) van die Wet
op Gevangenisse, 1959 (Wet no 8 van 1959) soos gewysig keur ek goed
dat spesiale afslag van vonnis aan die ondergenoemde gevangene
toegestaan word en dat hy op 11 Februarie 1990 vrygelaat is nadat
ingevolge artikel 69(2) van genoemde Wet gehandel is:

NELSON ROLIHLAHLA MANDELA

F. W. DE KLERK

STAATSPRESIDENT

Datum: 1990 -02- 0 9

H.J. COETSEE

MINISTER VAN DIE KABINET

19.1025.DK

The official release form signed by State President FW de Klerk, authorising Mandela's release.
It reads:

STATE PRESIDENT'S MINUTE NO: 110

**By virtue of the powers vested in me by section 69(1) of the Prisons Act, 1959 (Act no.8 of 1959) as
amended, I approve the special reduction of the sentence given to the prisoner mentioned below and
approve that he be released on 11 February 1990 after section 69(2) of the said Act has been followed:
NELSON ROLIHLAHLA MANDELA**

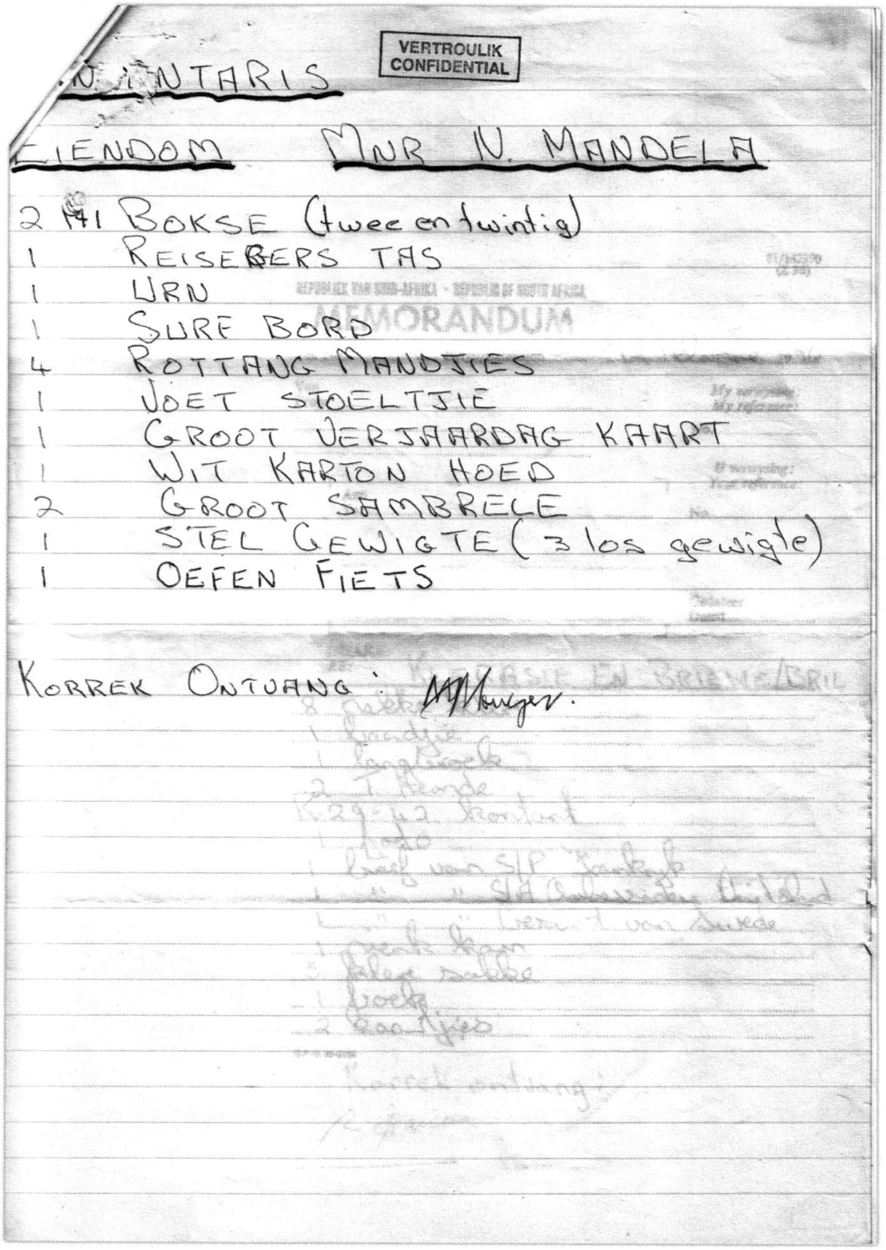

INVENTARIS

VERTROULIK
CONFIDENTIAL

EIENDOM   MNR N. MANDELA

2 1	BOKSE (twee en twintig)
1	REISEBERS TAS
1	URN
1	SURF BORD
4	ROTTANG MANDJIES
1	VOET STOELTJIE
1	GROOT VERJAARDAG KAART
1	WIT KARTON HOED
2	GROOT SAMBRELE
1	STEL GEWIGTE (3 los gewigte)
1	OEFEN FIETS

KORREK ONTVANG :

Inventory of Mandela's
personal items upon
his release.

On 9 February 1990, the Cabinet approved the order for the release of the world's longest-serving political prisoner. Records show that Nelson Mandela left with 22 boxes, a trunk, four baskets, an urn, a footstool, a cardboard hat, two large umbrellas, a set of exercise weights, an exercise bicycle, one giant birthday card, and a surfboard!

A DOCUMENT TO CREATE A CLIMATE OF UNDERSTANDING

MR PRESIDENT, I HOPE THAT MINISTERS KOBIE COETSEE AND GERRIT
VILJOEN HAVE INFORMED YOU THAT I DEEPLY APPRECIATE YOUR
DECISION IN TERMS OF WHICH EIGHT FELLOW PRISONERS WERE FREED
ON 15 OCTOBER 1989 AND FOR ADVISING ME OF THE FACT IN
ADVANCE.   THE RELEASE WAS CLEARLY A MAJOR DEVELOPMENT WHICH
RIGHTLY EVOKED PRAISE HERE AND ABROAD.

IN MY VIEW, IT HAS NOW BECOME URGENT TO TAKE OTHER MEASURES
TO END THE PRESENT DEADLOCK, AND THIS WILL CERTAINLY BE
ACHIEVED IF THE GOVERNMENT FIRST CREATES A PROPER CLIMATE
FOR NEGOTIATION FOLLOWED BY A MEETING WITH THE ANC.

THE CONFLICT WHICH IS PRESENTLY DRAINING SOUTH AFRICA'S
LIFEBLOOD, EITHER IN THE FORM OF PEACEFUL DEMONSTRATIONS,
ACTS OF VIOLENCE OR EXTERNAL PRESSURE WILL NEVER BE SETTLED
UNTIL THERE IS AN AGREEMENT WITH THE ANC. TO THIS END I
HAVE SPENT MORE THAN THREE YEARS URGING THE GOVERNMENT TO
NEGOTIATE WITH THE ANC. I HOPE I WILL NOT LEAVE THIS PLACE
WITH EMPTY HANDS.

THE GOVERNMENT INSISTS ON THE ANC MAKING AN HONEST
COMMITMENT TO PEACE BEFORE IT WILL TALK TO THE ORGANISATION.
THIS IS THE PRE-CONDITION WE ARE REQUIRED TO MEET BEFORE THE
GOVERNMENT WILL NEGOTIATE WITH US. IT MUST BE MADE CLEAR AT

December 1998 memorandum to State President FW de Klerk, in which Mandela reiterated
from his prison cell the ANC's preconditions for negotiation with the government.

THE OUTSET THAT THE ANC WILL NEVER MAKE SUCH A COMMITMENT AT
THE INSTANCE OF THE GOVERNMENT, OR OF ANY OTHER SOURCE FOR
THAT MATTER. WE WOULD HAVE THOUGHT THAT THE HISTORY OF THIS
COUNTRY'S LIBERATION MOVEMENT, ESPECIALLY DURING THE LAST 41
YEARS, WOULD HAVE MADE THAT POINT PERFECTLY CLEAR.

THE WHOLE APPROACH OF THE GOVERNMENT TO THE QUESTION OF
NEGOTIATION WITH THE ANC IS TOTALLY UNACCEPTABLE, AND
REQUIRES TO BE DRASTICALLY CHANGED. NO SERIOUS POLITICAL
ORGANISATION WILL EVER TALK PEACE WHEN AN AGGRESSIVE WAR IS
BEING WAGED AGAINST IT. NO PROUD PEOPLE WILL EVER OBEY
ORDERS FROM THOSE WHO HAVE HUMILIATED AND DISHONOURED THEM
FOR SO LONG.   BESIDES, THE PRE-CONDITION THAT WE SHOULD
COMMIT OURSELVES TO PEACE IS INCONSISTENT WITH THE STATEMENT
YOU MADE IN NIGEL SHORTLY BEFORE THE LAST GENERAL ELECTION,
IN WHICH YOU APPEALED TO BLACK LEADERS TO COME FORWARD TO
NEGOTIATE WITH THE GOVERNMENT AND TO REFRAIN FROM SETTING
PRE-CONDITIONS FOR SUCH NEGOTIATIONS. IT WAS GENERALLY
ASSUMED THAT THE APPEAL WAS ADDRESSED TO BLACKS AS A WHOLE
AND NOT, AS NOW APPEARS, ONLY TO THOSE WHO WORK IN APARTHEID
STRUCTURES.   IN THE LIGHT OF SUBSEQUENT GOVERNMENT POLICY
STATEMENTS, THE PERCEPTION HAS DEEPENDED THAT THE NIGEL
STATEMENT WAS NO MORE THAN MERE RHETORIC.   ALTHOUGH THE
GOVERNMENT CALLED ON BLACKS TO SET NO PRE-CONDITONS, IT
CONSIDERS ITSELF FREE TO DO EXACTLY THAT. THAT IS THE
REASON WHY IT PRESCRIBES TO US TO MAKE A COMMITMENT TO PEACE
BEFORE WE CAN TALK.

THE GOVERNMENT OUGHT TO BE AWARE THAT READINESS TO NEGOTIATE
IS IN ITSELF AN~~HAUNCH~~ *HONEST* COMMITMENT.   TO PEACE, IN THIS REGARD
THE ANC IS FAR AHEAD OF THE GOVERNMENT. IT HAS REPEATEDLY
DECLARED ITS WILLINGNESS TO NEGOTIATE, PROVIDED A PROPER
CLIMATE FOR SUCH NEGOTIATION EXISTS. THE ORGANISATION HAS
RECENTLY PUBLISHED A CLEAR AND DETAILED PLAN TO THIS EFFECT,
WHICH HAS ALREADY BEEN APPROVED BY THE FRONT LINE STATES
ORGANISATION OF AFRICAN UNITY, NON-ALIGNED MOVEMENT AND BY
ALMOST ALL THE MEMBERS OF THE COMMENWEALTH OF NATIONS.

EQUALLY RELEVANT IS THE FACT THAT ON MANY OCCASIONS IN THE
PAST THE ANC HAS EXPLICITLY ACKNOWLEDGED ITS COMMITMENT TO
PEACEFUL SOLUTIONS, IF CHANNELS FOR DOING SO ARE AVAILABLE.
AS RECENTLY AS 24 OCTOBER 1989 THE STAR REPORTED AS FOLLOWS:

"THE ANC SAYS IT IS COMMITTED TO A PEACEFUL SOLUTION IN
SOUTH AFRICA, BUT ACCUSES THE GOVERNMENT OF PRETORIA *RHETORIC.*
... AT PRESENT THERE IS REALLY NO SERIOUS INDICATION
FROM THE GOVERNEMENT ITSELF ABOUT A PEACEFUL SOLUTION
TO THE POLITICAL CRISIS ... FIVE YEARS AGO PRESIDENT P
W BOTHA SPOKE VIRTUALLY THE SAME WORDS, BUT NOTHING
HAPPENED.

IT IS HISTORY NOW THAT THE ANC HAS MADE IMPASSIONED
OVERTURES TO EVERY SINGLE GOVERNMENT OF SOUTH AFRICA IN
VAIN. EVERY MANOUVRE WAS MET WITH A NEGATIVE RESPONSE
AND AT TIMES VIOLENCE.".

4

THIS AND SIMILAR OTHER PREVIOUS STATEMENTS CLEARLY SHOW THAT
THE ANC HAS AN ESTABLISHED RECORD OF COMMITMENT TO PEACE,
AND THAT ITS ARMED STRUGGLE IS A PURELY DEFENSIVE MEASURE
AGAINST THE VIOLENCE OF THE GOVERNMENT.   THIS POINT WAS
STESSED BY MR OLIVER TAMBO, PRESIDENT OF THE ANC DURING AN
INVERVIEW WITH CAPE TIMES EDITOR, ANTHONY HEARD ON 4
NOVEMBER 1985, WHEN HE SAID:-

"THE UNFORTUNATE THING IS THAT PEOPLE LOVE *TEND* TO BE
WORRIED ABOUT THE VIOLENCE THAT OVERFLOW *COMES FROM* THE OPPRESSED
... REALLY THERE WOULD BE NO VIOLENCE AT ALL IF WE DID
NOT HAVE THE VIOLENCE OF THE APARTHEID SYSTEM.".

THERE IS NEITHER LOGIC NOR COMMON SENSE IN ASKING THE ANC TO
DO NOW WHAT IT HAS CONSISTENTLY DONE ON COUNTLESS OCCASIONS
BEFORE.   IT IS THE GOVERNMENT, NOT THE ANC THAT STARTED
CIVIL WAR IN THIS COUNTRY AND THAT DOES NOT WANT
RECONCILIATION AND PEACE.   HOW DOES ONE WORK FOR
RECONCILIATION AND PEACE UNDER A STATE OF EMERGENCY WITH
BLACK AREAS VIRTUALLY UNDER MILITARY OCCUPATION, WHEN
PEOPLES ORGANISATIONS ARE BANNED, LEADERS ARE EITHER IN
EXILE, PRISON OR RESTRICTED, WHEN THE POLICY OF APARTHEID,
WITH ALL ITS VIOLENCE, IS STILL BEING ENFORCED, AND WHEN NO
CONDITIONS FOR FREE POLITICAL EXPRESSION EXIST?

SERIOUS DOUBTS HAVE ALSO BEEN EXPRESSED AS TO WHETHER THE
GOVERNEMENT WOULD BE PREPARED TO MEET THE ANC EVEN WHEN IT

FULLY COMPLIED WITH YOUR DEMAND. POLITICAL COMMENTATORS
POINT OUT THAT DURING THE SERIES OF DISCUSSIONS YOU AND
OTHER GOVERNMENT MEMBERS HELD RECENTLY WITH THE "HOMELAND"
LEADERS AND THEIR URBAN COUNTERPARTS, YOU AVOIDED MEETING
THE VERY ORGANISATIONS WHICH, TOGETHER WITH THE ANC, HOLD
THE KEY TO PEACE IN THIS COUNTRY. THE UNITED DEMOCRATIC
FRONT AND ITS MAIN AFFILIATES, THE CONGRESS OF SOUTH AFRICAN
AND TRADE UNIONS, NATAL INDIAN CONGRESS AND TRANSVAAL INDIAN
CONGRESS, ARE ALL NON-VIOLENT AND PEACEFUL ORGINASATIONS.
WHY THEN DID THE GOVERNMENT IGNORE THEM IF COMMITMENT TO
PEACE IS THE ONLY QUALIFICATION FOR PARTICIPATION IN
NEGOTIATIONS?

IN YOUR INAUGURAL ADDRESS ON 20 SEPTEMBER 1989, YOU MADE AN
IMPORTANT STATEMENT WHICH MUST HAVE HAD A FORMIDABLE IMPACT
INSIDE AND OUTSIDE THE COUNTRY, YOU SAID:

> "THERE IS BUT ONE WAY TO PEACE, TO JUSTICE FOR ALL:
> THAT IS THE WAY OF RECONCILIATION, OF TOGETHER SEEKING
> MUTUALLY ACCEPTABLE SOLUTIONS; OF TOGETEHR DISCUSSING
> WHAT THE NEW SOUTH AFRICA COULD LOOK LIKE, OF
> CONSTITUTIONAL NEGOTIATION WITH A VIEW TO PERMANENT
> UNDERSTANDING.".

THE CORNERSTONE OF THAT ADDRESS WAS THE IDEA OF
RECONCILIATION IN WHICH YOU PLEADED FOR A NEW SPIRIT AND
APPROACH. BY RECONCILIATION, IN THIS CONTEXT, WAS

UNDERSTOOD THE SITUATION WHERE OPPONENTS, AND EVEN ENEMIES
FOR THAT MATTER, WOULD SINK THEIR DIFFERENCES AND LAY DOWN
ARMS FOR THE PURPOSE OF WORKING OUT A PEACEFUL SOLUTION,
WHERE THE INJUSTICES AND GRIEVANCES OF THE PAST WOULD BE
BURIED AND FORGOTTEN AND A FRESH START MADE. THAT IS THE
SPIRIT IN WHICH THE PEOPLE OF SOUTH AFRICA WOULD LIKE TO
WORK TOGETHER FOR PEACE; THOSE ARE THE PRINCIPLES WHICH
SHOULD GUIDE THOSE WHO LOVE THEIR COUNTRY AND ITS PEOPLE;
WHO WANT TO TURN SOUTH AFRICA INTO A LAND OF HOPE. IN
HIGHLIGHTING THIS THEME IN YOUR ADDRESS, YOU SPARKED OFF A
GROUNDSWELL OF EXPECTATIONS FROM FAR AND WIDE. MANY PEOPLE
FELT THAT, AT LAST, THE SOUTH AFRICA OF THEIR DREAMS WAS
ABOUT TO BE BORN.

WE ALSO UNDERSTOOD YOUR APPEAL FOR RECONCILIATION AND
JUSTICE FOR ALL, NOT TO BE DIRECTED TO THOSE BLACKS WHO
OPERATE APARTHEID STRUCTURES. APART FROM A FEW NOTABLE
EXCEPTIONS, THESE BLACKS ARE THE CREATION OF THE NATIONAL
PARTY AND THROUGHOUT THE YEARS, THEY HAVE SERVED AS ITS
LOYAL AGENTS IN ITS VARIOUS STRATEGIES TO CLING TO MINORITY
RULE. THEIR PRINCIPAL ROLE HAS BEEN, AND STILL IS, TO MAKE
THE STRUGGLE FOR MAJORITY RULE IN A UNITARY STATE FAR MORE
DIFFICULT TO ACHIEVE. FOR THE LAST THREE DECADES THEY HAVE
BEEN USED TO DEFEND THE NP'S POLICY OF GROUP DOMINATION -
NOW REFERRED TO AS GROUP RIGHTS - AND THEY HAVE NO TRADITION
OF MILITANT RESISTANCE AGAINST RACIAL DISCRIMINATION. THERE

IS THUS NO CONFLICT TO BE RECONCILED BETWEEN THE NP AND
THESE PEOPLE.

THE APPEAL COULD NOT HAVE BEEN DIRECTED TO ANY OF THE
OPPOSITION PARTIES IN PARLIAMENT EITHER. ALTHOUGH THE NP
HAS MADE POSITIVE INITIATIVES HERE AND THERE, ITS PUBLIC
IMAGE IS STILL TARNISHED BY A CLOUD OF DISTRUST AND
SUSPICION AND BY AN INHERENT VAGUENESS AND INDECISION AS FAR
AS THE REALLY BASIC ISSUES ARE CONCERNED. MANY PEOPLE SEE
NO FUNDAMENTAL DIFFERENCE BETWEEN ITS POLICIES AND THOSE OF
THE CONSERVATIVE PARTY. BOTH ARE REGARDED AS APARTHEID
PARTIES, THE ONLY DIFFERENCE BEING THAT ONE IS MORE BLUNT
THAT THE OTHER IN ITS DEFENCE OF WHITE PRIVILEGE.

ALTHOUGH THE DEMOCRATIC PARTY IS THE MOST PROGRESSIVE
PARLIAMENTARY PARTY, AND DESPITE THE EXISTENCE OF IMPORTANT
POLICY DIFFERENCES BETWEEN THAT PARTY AND THE NP, THE
RELATIONS BETWEEN THE TWO PARTIES ARE NOT SO BITTER AS TO
JUSTIFY A CALL FOR RECONCILIATION AND PEACE BY A HEAD OF
STATE. THE FAIRLY EVEN RELATIONS BETWEEN THE TWO PARTIES IS
CLEARLY ILLUSTRATED BY THE FACT THAT THE DP IS NOT BANNED,
NONE OF ITS LEADERS ARE RESTRICTED, IMPRISONED, DRIVEN TO
EXILE OR EXECUTED FOR PURELY POLITICAL OFFENCES, AS IS
HAPPENING TO OUR PEOPLE.

THE CONFLICT WHICH WE BELIEVED YOU WANTED TO SETTLE WAS THAT
BETWEEN THE GOVERNMENT ON THE ONE HAND, AND THE ANC AND

OTHER EXTRA-PARLIAMENTARY ORGANISATIONS, ON THE OTHER HAND.
IT IS THE ACTIVITIES OF THESE ORGANISATIONS WHICH HAVE
TURNED SOUTH AFRICA INTO A LAND OF ACUTE TENSIONS AND FEAR.
IT IS ON THIS LEVEL THAT THE COUNTRY DESPERATELY YEARNS FOR
RECONCILIATION AND JUSTICE FOR ALL. AS POINTED OUT ON
ANOTHER OCCASION, DIALOGUE WITH THE ANC AND THE MASS
DEMOCRATICE MOVEMENT IS THE ONLY WAY OF STOPPING VIOLENCE
AND BRINGING PEACE TO THE COUNTRY. IT IS, THEREFORE,
IRONICAL THAT IT IS PRECISELY THESE ORGANISATIONS WITH WHOM
THE GOVERNMENT IS NOT AT ALL PREPARED TO TALK.

IT IS COMMON KNOWLEDGE THAT THE GOVERNMENT HAS BEEN SHARPLY
CRITICISED AND EVEN CONDEMNED IN THE PAST FOR SQUANDERING
PREVIOUS RESOURCES AND FOR WASTING MUCH ENERGY AND TIME
DISCUSSING WITH PEOPLE WHO CAN PLAY NO SIGNIFICANT ROLE IN
THE RESOLUTION OF THE CURRENT CONFLICT IN THE COUNTRY.
PAST EXPERIENCE SHOWS THAT THE GOVERNMENT WOULD PREFER TO
MAKE PEACE WITH THOSE WHO ACCEPT ITS POLICIES, RATHER THAN
THOSE WHO REJECT THEM, WITH ITS FRIENDS RATHER THAN WITH ITS
OPPONENTS. IT IS TO BE HOPED THAT THIS TIME THE GOVERNMENT
WILL NOT REPEAT THAT COSTLY MISTAKE. TO CONTINUE TO IGNORE
THIS CRITICISM, AND TO CONFINE CONSULTATIONS ON THE
POLITICAL CRISES ALMOST ENTIRELY TO THOSE INDIVIDUALS AND
ORGANISATIONS WHICH HELP THE GOVERNMENT TO MAINTAIN THE
STATSU QUO, WILL CERTAINLY DEEPEN THE DISTRUST AND SUSPICION
WHICH IMPEDES REAL PROGRESS ON NEGOTIATIONS. IN MY
LENGTHY DISCUSSIONS WITH THE TEAM OF GOVERNMENT OFFICIALS, I

9

REPEATEDLY URGED THAT NEGOTIATIONS BETWEEN THE ANC AND THE
GOVERNMENT SHOULD PREFERABLY BE IN TWO STAGES. THE FIRST
BEING WHERE THE GOVERNMENT AND THE ANC WOULD TOGETHER WORK
OUT THE PRE-CONDITIONS FOR NEGOTIATIONS. THE SECOND STAGE
WOULD CONSIST OF THE ACTUAL NEGOTIATIONS THEMSELVES WHEN THE
CLIMATE FOR DOING SO WAS RIPE. THESE WERE MY PERSONAL VIEWS
AND NOT THOSE OF THE ANC WHICH SEES THE PROBLEM QUITE
DIFFERENTLY. IT SEEMS TO ME THAT NOW THAT I AM AWARE OF THE
ATTITUDE OF THE ANC ON THE MATTER, AN ATTITUDE WHICH IS
PERFECTLY SOUND, WE SHOULD WORK ON THE FORMULA INDICATED BY
THE ORGANISATION FOR THE RESOLUTION OF THE PRESENT OBSTACLES
TO NEGOTIATION.

THE PRINCIPLE SOURCE OF ALMOST ALL OUR PROBLEMS IN THIS
COUNTRY IS UNDOUBTEDLY THE POLICY OF APARTHEID, WHICH THE
GOVERNMENT NOW ADMITS IS AN UNJUST SYSTEM, AND FROM WHICH IT
CLAIMS TO BE MOVING AWAY. THIS MEANS THAT ORGANISATIONS AND
PEOPLE WHO WERE BANNED, RESTRICTED, DRIVEN INTO EXILE,
IMPRISONED OR EXECUTED FOR THEIR ANTI-APARTHEID ACTIVITIES
WERE UNJUSTLY CONDEMNED. THE VERY FIRST STEP ON THE WAY TO
RECONCILIATION IS OBVIOUSLY THE DISMANTLING OF APARTHEID AND
ALL MEASURES USED TO ENFORCE IT. TO TALK OF RECONCILIATION
BEFORE THIS MAJOR STEP IS TAKEN IS TOTALLY UNREALISTIC.

THE FIVE-YEAR PLAN OF THE NP, WITH ITS OUTDATED CONCEPT OF
GROUP RIGHTS, HAS AGGRAVATED THE POSITION ALMOST BEYOND
REPAIR. IT IS YET ANOTHER EXAMPLE OF THE GOVERNMENT'S

ATTEMPT "TO MODERNISE APARTHEID WITHOUT ABANDONING IT".
WHAT THE PLAN IN EFFECT MEANS IS THAT, AFTER RESISTING
RACIAL OPPRESSION FOR SO MANY YEARS AND AFTER MAKING SUCH
HEAVY SACRIFICES DURING WHICH COUNTLESS LIVES HAVE BEEN
LOST, WE SHOULD AT THE HEIGHT OF THAT HEROIC STRUGGLE YIELD
TO A DISGUISED FORM OF MINORITY RULE. IN A NUTSHELL, THE
PLAN MEANS THAT BLACKS WILL TASTE REAL FREEDOM ONLY IN THE
WORLD TO COME. IN THIS ONE WHITES WILL GO ON PREACHING
RECONCILIATION AND PEACE, BUT CONTINUE TO HOLD FIRMLY AND
DEFAULTY TO POWER, TO ENFREE RACIAL SEPERATION. THE VERY
ISSUES WHICH HAVE CAUSED SO MUCH AGONY AND BITTERNISS IN THE
COUNTRY. INSISTENCE ON SUCH A PLAN WILL RENDER MEANINGLESS
ALL TALK OF "RECONCILIATION AND JUSTICE FOR ALL, OF TOGETHER
SEEKING MUTUALLY ACCEPTABLE SOLUTIONS OF TOGETHER DISCUSSING
WHAT THE NEW SOUTH AFRICA SHOULD BE LIKE OF CONSTITUTIONAL
NEGOTIATION WITH A VIEW TO A PERMANENT UNDERSTANDING".

WE EQUALLY REJECT OUT OF HAND THE GOVERNMENT'S PLAN TO HOLD
RACIALLY BASED ELECTIONS TO DETERMINE THOSE WHO SHOULD TAKE
PART IN NEGOTIATIONS. COMMENTATORS OF DIFFERENT POLITICAL
VIEWS CONSIDER IT ABSURD FOR THE GOVERNMENT TO ADVOCATE
ESSENTIALLY RACIST PROCEDURES, WHERE THE OVERWHELMING
MAJORITY OF THE POPULATION IS STRIVING FOR A NON-RACIAL
SYSTEM OF GOVERNMENT.

THE GOVERNMENT ARGUES TAHT OUR SITUATION IS A COMPLEX ONE,
AND THAT A LASTING SOLUTION WILL ONLY BE FOUND AFTER YEARS

OF CONSULTATION AND PLANNING.   WE TOTALLY REJECT THAT VIEW.
THERE IS NOTHING DUPLICATED IN REPLACING MINORITY RULE WITH
MAJORITY RULE, GROUP DOMINATION WITH A NON-RACIAL SOCIAL
ORDER. THE POSITION IS DUPLICATED SIMPLY BECAUSE THE
GOVERNMENT ITSELF IS NOT YET READY TO ACCEPT THE MOST
OBVIOUS SOLUTION WHICH THE MAJORITY DEMANDS, AND BELIEVES
THAT A RACIAL SOLUTION CAN STILL BE IMPOSED ON THE COUNTRY.

THE GOVERNEMENT CLAIMS THAT THE ANC IS NOT THE SOLE
REPRESENTATIVE OF BLACK ASPIRATIONS IN THIS COUNTRY,
THEREFORE, IT (THE GOVERNMENT) CANNOT BE EXPECTED TO HAVE
SEPARATE DISCUSSIONS WITH THE ORGANISATION. IT CAN ONLY DO
SO IN THE PRESENCE OF OTHER ORGANISATIONS. WE REJECT THESE
ARGUMENTS AS YET ANOTHER EXAMPLE OF THE GOVERNMENT'S
INTRANSIGENCE ALL THOSE WHO RESORT TO SUCH AN ARGUMENT MAKE
THEMSELVES WIDE OPEN TO THE CHARGE OF USING DOUBLE
STANDARDS. IS IS NOW PUBLIC KNOWLEDGE THAT THE GOVERNEMENT
HAS ON NUMEROUS OCCASIONS HELD SEPARATE DISCUSSIONS WITH
EACH OF THE "HOMELAND" LEADERS AND WITH THEIR URBAN
COURTERPARTS. FOR THE GOVERNEMENT NOW TO REFUSE US THIS
PRIVILEGE WOULD NOT ONLY BE INCONSISTENT WITH ITS OWN
ACTIONS, BUT THAT WOULD SERIOUSLY UNDERMINE THE
CONFIDENCE-BUILDING EXERCISE ON WHICH WE HAVE EMBARKED,
COMPELLING ALL THOSE INVOLVED TO SEEK MUTUALLY ACCEPTABLE
SOLUTIONS UNDER VERY GRAVE DIFFICULTIES. EQUALLY IMPORTANT
IS THE FACT THAT THERE IS WAR BETWEEN THE ANC AND THE
GOVERNMENT AND A CEASEFIRE TO END HOSTILITIES WILL HAVE TO

12

BE NEGOTIATED FIRST BEFORE TALKS TO NORMALISE THE SITUATION
CAN BEGIN.   ONLY THE GOVERNMENT AND THE ANC AND ITS ALLIES
CAN TAKE PART IN SUCH TALKS AND NO THIRD PARTY WOULD BE
NEEDED.   I MUST NOW REFER TO A DIFFERENT BUT RELATED MATTER
WHICH I HOPE WILL RECEIVE YOUR URGENT ATTENTION, THAT IS THE
RELEASE OF FOUR FELLOW PRISONERS WHO WERE SENTENCED TO LIFE
IMPRISONMENT BY A NATAL COURT IN 1978 AND WHO ARE PRESENTLY
HELD ON ROBBEN ISLAND.   THEY ARE:

1.   MR MATTHEW MEYIWA   :   (66 YEARS)

2.   MR ELPHAS MDLALOSE   :   (66 YEARS)

3.   MR ANTHONY XABA   :   (56 YEARS)

4.   JOHN NENE   :   (+ 56 YEARS)

THEY WERE FIRST SENTENCED IN 1964.   MR MDLALOSE TO 10
YEARS IMPRISONMENT AND THE REST TO EIGHT YEARS.   IN 1978
THEY WERE AGAIN CONVICTED AND SENTENCED, THIS TIME TO LIFE
IMPRISONMENT.   FOR REASONS WHICH WERE CAREFULLY EXPLAINED
TO MINISTERS GERRIT VILJOEN AND KOBIE COETSEE ON 10 OCTOBER
1989, AND TO THE GOVERNMENT TEAM ON 16 NOVEMBER 1989.   I
HAD EXPECTED MESSRS MDLALOSE AND MEYWE TO BE FREED TOGETHER
WITH THE EIGHT FELLOW PRISONERS MENTIONED ABOVE.   I WAS
INDEED EXTREMELY DISTRESSED WHEN THE TWO WERE NOT INCLUDED.
BEARING IN MIND ALL THE SURROUNDING CIRCUMSTANCES TO THE
CASE, THE FACT THAT THESE FOUR PERSONS ARE NOT FIRST
OFFENDERS SHOULD BE REGARDED AS A MITIGATING, AND NOT AS AN
AGGRAVATING FACTOR.

I WOULD LIKE TO BELIEVE THAT MY EXPLORATORY EFFORTS DURING
THE LAST THREE YEARS HAVE NOT BEEN IN VAIN, THAT I HAVE AN
IMPORTANT ROLE STILL TO PLAY IN HELPING TO BRING ABOUT A
PEACEFUL SETTLEMENT THAT THE INITIATIVES YOU HAVE ALREADY
TAKEN WILL SOON BE FOLLOWED BY OTHER DEVELOPMENTS ON THE
REALLY FUNDAMENTAL ISSUE THAT ARE AGITATING OUR PEOPLE AND
THAT IN OUR LIFETIME OUR COUNRTRY WILL RID ITSELF OF THE
PESTILENCE OF RACIALISM IN ALL ITS FORMS.

IN CONCLUSION, MR PRESIDENT, I SHOULD ADD THAT IN HELPING TO
PROMOTE DIALOGUE BETWEEN THE ANC AND THE GOVERNEMENT, I HOPE
TO BE ABLE TO AVOID ANY ACT WHICH MAY BE INTERPRETED AS AN
ATTEMPT ON MY PART TO DRIVE A WEDGE BETWEEN YOU AND THE NP,
OR TO PORTRAY YOU IN A MANNER NOT CONSISTENT WITH YOUR
PUBLIC IMAGE. I TRUST THAT YOU AND OTHER MEMBERS OF THE
GOVERNMENT WILL FULLY RECIPROCATE.

The Rivonia trialists meet at Victor Verster in 1989 under the tree that was bugged by National Intelligence.

CHAPTER FIVE

Walking in Freedom

The end of one story is the beginning of another

In the run-up to Mandela's release in February 1990, intense attention was given to the icon who had not been seen for 27 years. What would he look like? With the aid of descriptions provided by recently released fellow-inmates and photographs of Mandela taken in the early 1960s, an artist prepared an identikit portrait that featured on the release posters, and mutated into countless further iterations. Excitement reached fever pitch the moment he walked through the gates of Victor Verster prison.

The world was astonished by the difference in appearance between the man who had entered prison and the man who emerged. The archive of the prison experience was inscribed in his person, etched on his body, profoundly shaping his consciousness and embedded in his unconscious (so much so that when Mandela built a house in his hometown of Qunu after his release, he modelled it on his prison bungalow at Victor Verster!).

The prison experience almost certainly accompanied Mandela into the complex negotiations for the transfer of power and the fraught processes of national reconciliation. Things could not be otherwise because it had helped shape the man he had become – it was within him. Of course, it is impossible to determine with any accuracy the extent to which his years in prison had moulded Mandela's approach to the post-1990 transition in South Africa, but many of the well-practised prison strategies documented here were clearly discernible.

The Prison Archive focuses a uniquely intimate lens on the man best known for his public roles. Through its documents, the observer is privy to his anxieties, his longings and his passions – a first-hand experience of the complex entanglements of personal and political considerations negotiated by the father, husband, lawyer and leader. In this encounter with the Prison Archive, it is possible, for example, to trace the human thread that flows from the letters to his own beloved children to those to his jailer's wife and child.

Prison is designed to be a bounded space of control, but even prison cannot confine the energy contained within the archive. Mandela's Prison Archive is bursting with story. It contains intimate details of the prisoner's daily life, desires and concerns.

OPPOSITE:

An artist's impression of Mandela before his release.

It holds stories of ongoing personal and political development, and brims with tales of pragmatism and principle in complex combinations. It chronicles decades of struggle and negotiation between prisoners and captors, from the most coercive to the most diplomatic. The Prison Archive also reveals how all of this changed over time, closely following the world outside, a world from which the prison was designed to be sealed off.

The prison dresses its inmates in prison garb – during the early years of incarceration, Mandela wore the short pants he recognised were designed to demote him to the status of a 'boy' – and the warders in uniforms. It seeks, through these signals and countless other practices, to separate the 'wrongdoers' from the 'agents of justice', and to bring about the rehabilitation of the former through the custody of the latter. It is in the Prison Archive that these very categories are challenged, where warders such as Christo Brand accepted an invitation to rethink the nature of justice and humanity.

The prisoners were required to labour first at the breaking of stones and, from 1965, in the lime quarry. Later came the collecting of seaweed. It was desultory labour, forced from them. Then, in 1977, during the state-sponsored media visit to Robben Island, the authorities foregrounded a form of seemingly productive labour – gardening. The prisoners, however, resisted the propaganda agenda of the visit, and wrested control over the symbol of garden labour. While the 1977 images were a charade, by then gardening had become an important activity for Nelson Mandela and some of the other prisoners. They nurtured their own garden, from which, characteristically, they sustained not only themselves, but also the warders, with choice items.

'A garden was one of the few things in prison that one could control,' wrote Mandela. Much of his correspondence with the authorities reveals the adroit ways in which he extended his influence from the tiny patch of soil in the corner of a courtyard to the entire prison, the other inmates and the warders, his many connections beyond the prison walls, the apartheid state, and ultimately the world.

'Mr Mandela is our chief gardener,' wrote Ahmed Kathrada in a letter to Rookie Saloojee on 24 December 1976, 'and he takes his work very seriously' (Ahmed Kathrada, *Letters from Robben Island*, Mayibuye Books / Robben Island Museum, Cape Town, 1999, page 78). Someone somewhere recognised the power contained in that seemingly innocuous line. Rookie never got to read it as it was censored out of the letter at the time. But it bubbled up out of the archive, as suppressions and secrets regularly do in all archives, when Kathrada published his prison correspondence.

OPPOSITE:

Mandela's bungalow at Victor Verster (top) and his first house in Qunu following his release.

The prisoners' own garden was enormously productive, yielding thousands of chillies and tomatoes, among other produce. The garden was a fitting metaphor for the alternative system of morality, discipline and education that the prisoners nurtured, and that in turn sustained them. It was a harvest that they shared with the rest of South Africa when they walked out to freedom – a harvest that demonstrated, in a profound sense, that they had always been walking in freedom.

Tomatoes ripening on the bookcase in Mandela's cell.

Minister Kobie Coetsee gives Mandela a briefcase as a gift before his release from Victor Verster. Between the two of them is Niël Barnard, head of the National Intelligence Service.

Sources and Permissions

Front Cover: National Archives
End Papers: National Archives
Title Page: Robben Island Museum
(photographer Matthew Willman)
Table of Contents: Robben Island Museum
(photographer Matthew Willman)
Back Cover: Nelson Mandela Foundation
(photographer Matthew Willman)

Bailey's African History Archive
Page 104 (photographer Alf Kumalo)
(with thanks to Jacqui Masiza)

Gail Behrman
Pages 138-145, 154 and 206
(filmmaker David Oosthuizen and transcript
by David A Wallace, with thanks to Jan
Jansen, the South African Broadcasting
Corporation, and Ingrid Gavshon)

Christo Brand
Page 171

Brenthurst Library: Percy Yutar Papers
Pages 59, 61-63 and 114
(with thanks to Diana Madden)

The Bulletin: Australia
Page 84 (with thanks to Gail Behrman)

Donald Card
Page 111

Benny Gool
Pages 26 and 27

Alf Kumalo
Pages 80 and 82

Mac Maharaj
Pages 13 and 177 (with thanks to the Nelson
Mandela Museum, Mthatha)

National Archives
Pages 28-34, 53, 71-76, 81, 86, 88-90, 129-
131, 133, 135, 137, 146-150, 152-153, 156-
157, 160, 163, 173, 175, 178-183, 185-201,
204 (top) and 207
(with thanks to Zahira Adams, Natalie
Skomolo and Gerrit Wagener)

National Geographic
Page 158 (photographer Raghubir Singh)
(with thanks to Bart Luirink)

Nelson Mandela Foundation
Pages 38, 44, 46-49, 67 (donated by Ahmed
Kathrada), 70, 101, 105, 107, 151, 161-162,
164-169 and 205 (below)

Nelson Mandela Foundation
Photographer Gutto Bussab
Pages 40, 50-51, 64, 120-124 and 126-127

Nelson Mandela Foundation
Photographer Matthew Willman
Pages 8, 10, 12, 14-17, 92-96, 108, 117-119
and 159

Netherlands Institute for Southern Africa
Page 202 (with thanks to Kier Schuringa)

Reuters
Pages 42 and 43

**Robben Island Museum
Mayibuye Centre / University of
the Western Cape**
Pages 78-79, 102 (photographer
Eli Weinberg) and 113 (above)
(with thanks to Graham Goddard)

**Robben Island Museum
Photographer Matthew Willman**
Pages 18, 20, 22, 24, 45, 91, 99 and 170

South African Broadcasting Corporation
Page 113 (left)
(with thanks to Sias Scott)

Douw Steyn
Pages 56 and 57

Truth and Reconciliation Commission
Page 54 (photographer Gutto Bussab)
(with thanks to the South African History
Archive)

Umlando Wezithombe
Pages 36 and 39
(with thanks to Nic Buchanan)

**University of the Witwatersrand
Historical Papers**
Page 68
(Rivonia Trial records)
(with thanks to Michele Pickover)